DIVE Sᴛ ABBS
ᴀɴᴅ EYEMOUTH

A DIVER GUIDE

Lawson Wood

Underwater World Publications

Above: Salvage diver getting ready to start work on the wreck of the
Alfred Earlandsen (Site **26**).
Title page: Overlooking St Abbs harbour.
Front cover: Diver in gully at St Abbs. *Inset:* Wolf fish – synonymous with
diving in this area.

Editorial production by Martyn Yeo and Rebecca Bomford

Map artwork by Meena Arnold

Produced by Diver Magazine

Published by Underwater World Publications Ltd, 55 High Street, Teddington,
Middlesex, TW11 8HA

First published 1998

ISBN 0 946020 27 2

Printed in the United Arab Emirates by Emirates Printing Press,
PO Box 5106, Airport Road, Dubai

FOREWORD

by David Bellamy

When you want to experience the true wonder of Earth's own inner space, there is only one thing better to do than reading one of Lawson Wood's guides, and that is to go diving with him. He is not only a master at the art of underwater photography but a master at the craft of interpreting the complexities of the underwater world, and especially of our interaction with it. Like so many other divers, I had some of my first and best dives at St Abbs and I have been privileged to dive there with Lawson as a buddy and guide. Now you can do the same.

St Abbs has an important role in the history of underwater conservation. The resolve of the Marine Reserve played a central part in the designation of the whole of the Berwickshire coast, and most of the Northumberland coast, as a special area of conservation. The kelp beds are amazing, the fish and fishing communities friendly, the seabirds spectacular and the invertebrates, sea stars, molluscs, crustaceans and worms absolutely fascinating. Local hospitality in caravan parks, guest houses and hotels is excellent and the Borders countryside is without equal. No wonder it is a great place to dive. So dry suits on, leave only ripples, take only photographs, led by who else – Lawson Wood.

*This guide is dedicated to the crews of the
St Abbs and Eyemouth lifeboats, who are
unswerving in their duty along the south-east coast
of Scotland. Without their help many of us would not
be here today to continue diving in the St Abbs and
Eyemouth Voluntary Marine Nature Reserve*

CONTENTS

Diver and lion's mane jellyfish.

HOW TO USE THIS GUIDE

The Berwickshire coast has long been regarded as one of the top diving areas of the world and as representing the best of British diving. The selection in this guide starts at Berwick-upon-Tweed – because it offers some good freshwater sites when access for seaward sites is "blown out" by bad weather – and includes all the popular sites off Burnmouth, Eyemouth and the rest of the Marine Reserve. It continues up the coast to Fast Castle Head, which is probably as far as it is wise to venture in an RIB or hard boat from St Abbs or Eyemouth. There are some excellent wrecks, reefs and shore dives off Dunbar, but the area is beyond the remit of this book and has already been extensively covered by Gordon Ridley in the companion volume *Dive Scotland Volume III*.

Dive sites

Dive sites are listed from south to north. If your favourite dive or wreck site has been left out it should be stressed that this book is only a guide – there are hundreds of potential sites all the way along this coastline, which is well worth exploring. In fact, the entire area is so rich in marine life that the efforts of the Marine Reserve have finally been recognised and rewarded. The whole of Berwickshire and most of Northumberland have been designated a Special Area of Conservation by the European Union.

The locations described in the book have been split into four distinct areas, within which the sites included are regarded as some of the most popular for access, marine life content, interest, location and services available. These four areas all have distinct ecosystems and yield a huge variety of marine life, wrecks and staggering underwater, as well as topside, scenery. For each area there is a general description, and details of the various coastal features, wrecks and dive sites of interest. There are also simplified route instructions, descriptions of launch sites, details of any historical interest and an indication of the diving expertise required.

Wherever they are diving, exploratory divers should always consult with the Admiralty Tidal Stream Atlas, Ordnance Survey maps, the local Coastguard and, if possible, should collect accurate up-to-date information from local contacts such as dive shops and other divers. Locations given in this guide have been standardised to Ordnance Survey map sheets. All the latitude and longitude co-ordinates (shown not in metric form but in degrees, minutes and seconds) were taken with a hand-held GPS, allowing publication for the first time of concise and exact location marks for the dive sites listed. The most up-to-date knowledge possible is provided to enable divers to enhance their skills considerably and also to save them valuable searching time.

MAPS AND CHARTS

The following maps and charts are relevant to the area covered by this guide:

Admiralty Chart 160 – St Abbs Head to Farne Islands

Admiralty Chart 175 – Fife Ness to St Abbs

Admiralty Chart 1047 – Montrose to Berwick-upon-Tweed

Admiralty Chart 1192 – St Abbs Head to River Tyne

Admiralty Chart 1612 – Harbours and Anchorages

OS Pathfinder 423 map sheet NT 86/96 (1:25,000)

OS Pathfinder 438 map sheet NT 95/NU 05 (1:25,000)

Four waterproofed reference maps by the author, available from dive shops in the area

Admiralty Charts can be obtained from Lilly & Gillie at North Shields (tel. 0191 258 3519).

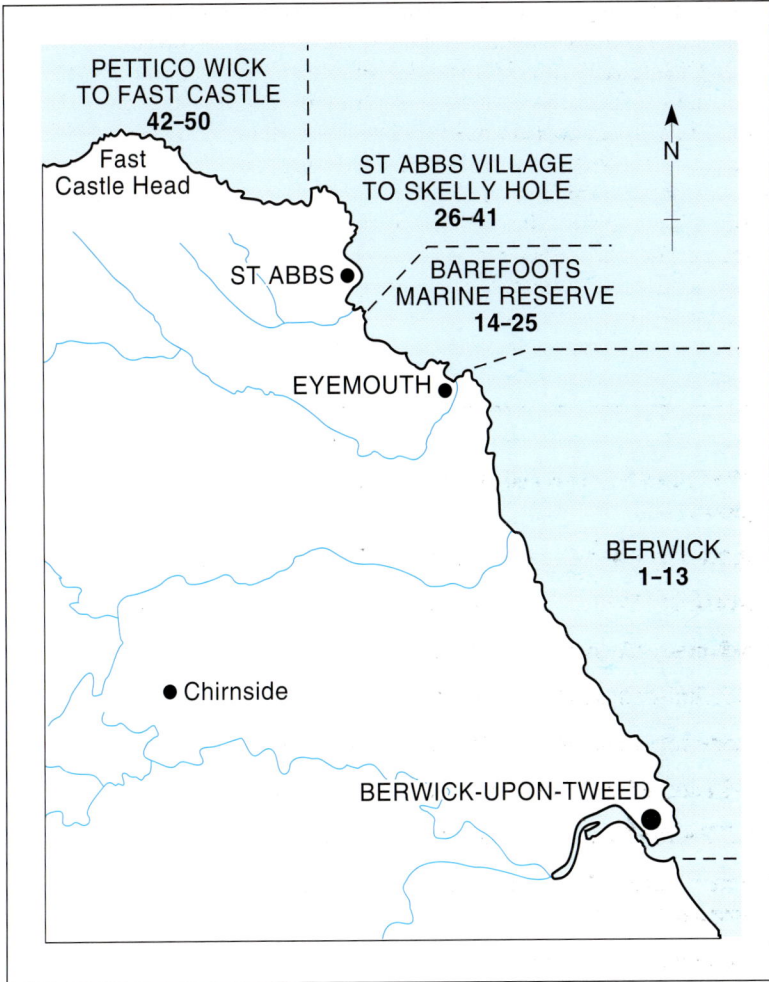

The four areas covered by this guide.

ABOUT THE BERWICKSHIRE COAST

The Berwickshire shore is a vast, rugged and diverse landscape that encompasses inter-tidal sea caves, submarine reefs, interesting wrecks and an abundance of marine life. The nature of the land is such that there are few easily accessible shore entry sites and slipways, so all the diving tends to be concentrated in a few places.

The astounding diversity of marine life and the unspoiled scenery are just a small part of what Scotland can offer visitors on diving holidays. Just over the Firth of Forth in North Queensferry, nestled under the famous Forth Bridge, is Deep Sea World, the largest salt-water marine aquarium in Europe, featuring Scottish marine life. The Scottish Borders, with their many abbeys and castles, are just a short drive away and in Eyemouth there is a new multi-million pound marine interpretive centre, under construction at the time of writing (*see* Site **12**). Local facilities include road and rail links, accommodation of varying types and standards, equipment sales and hire, boat hire, launching facilities, compressors, instruction, wrecks, photography and nature reserves.

Diving the Berwickshire coastline can be an exhilarating experience – the underwater life is exceptionally profuse, there are many exciting wrecks and the underwater cliffs and caves are tremendous. There is an almost total lack of "diver pollution", except at one or two of the most popular sites, and then only during peak holiday time.

The dives within the confines of the Marine Reserve range from easy, gently sloping shore dives to challenging drift dives in difficult tidal conditions. There are little-dived major wrecks and many relatively undiscovered and undived wreck sites enticingly marked on the Admiralty charts (though some are very deep and beyond the range of most sport divers, there is a new technical diving operation based in Eyemouth that is able to supply mixed gas systems for those qualified to use them). Divers who want to explore the coastline away from normal diving activities to some of the deeper wrecks enticingly recorded on the Admiralty charts should get in touch with the local Coastguard first.

Opposite: Common seal on the rocks at Fast Castle Head.

The coastline is dramatic and rugged, with canyons and caves all the way along. The sea bed is generally covered with large boulders, falling away to gravel and sand at about the 20m zone. The exposed cliff faces are renowned for the great diversity of marine life and are festooned with soft corals, brilliantly coloured anemones, hydroids, tunicates, fish and crustaceans. There are large boulder-strewn areas where ballan wrasse (*Labrus bergylta*) eat out of your hand and where wolf fish try to eat the rest of your hand! The predominant feature is the kelp forest that fringes much of the coast, grazed by sea urchins and home to spider crabs, nudibranchs and blennies. Farther offshore are brittlestar beds with giant dahlias and plumose anemones, the rare Arctic anemone (*Bolocera tuediae*), burrowing anemones (*Cerianthus lloydi*) and huge angler fish. Octopus and squid are common on night dives and the rare Yarrel's blenny (*Chirolophis ascanii*) is not rare here among the gullies, canyons and caves that cut through the headlands. For more detail, read the chapter on Marine Life.

It would be remiss not to mention the freshwater diving in the area. All the lochs are accessible but very deep, silty and rather dull, as well as being several hours' drive from the coast. However, diving in the rivers and deep pools is an interesting alternative. The River Tweed near Kelso, Norham and Coldstream, for instance, has generally clear water and there is a good chance to encounter trout and salmon as they swim upstream to the spawning grounds.

The mouth of the River Tweed also offers an alternative site when the

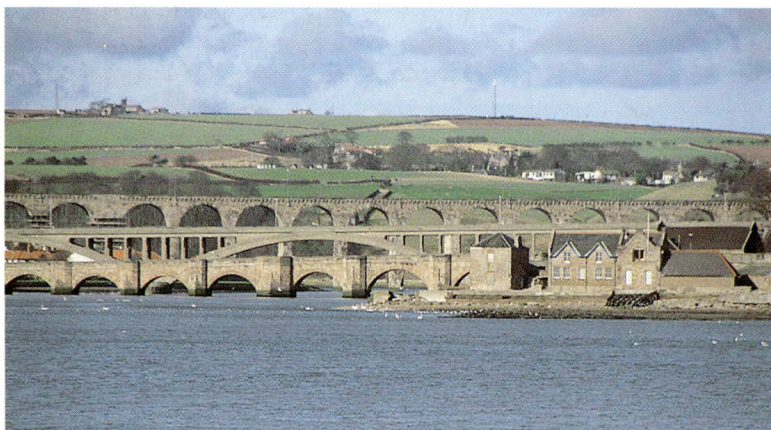

The three bridges, Berwick-upon-Tweed.

sea is too rough. During an incoming tide, when the current is less strong, diving under the Old Bridge at Berwick-upon-Tweed (Site 1) is particularly interesting with mussel beds, blennies, gobies and flounders (*Platichthys flesus*). Similarly, the rivers – Eye, Blackadder and Whitadder – have some deep pools that are also very interesting and all filled with the common eel, which makes its annual migration via the Gulf Stream from the Sargasso Sea. The south-east coast of Scotland is for the exploratory diver, so try the rivers too – you will not be disappointed, and remember to check with the local tourist board to find out whether special permission is required, particularly during the fishing season.

How to get there

By air Visitors to St Abbs and Eyemouth may fly to Edinburgh or Newcastle upon Tyne. Car rentals are available from each of these airports, as are links for the train. Pick-up can also be arranged in advance from a few of the dive centres.

By road Travel up the east coast along the A1 trunk road. When you reach Berwick-upon-Tweed turn left at the roundabout by the Safeway supermarket and continue along the A1 until you cross into Scotland. Then turn right along the A1107 to Eyemouth, just 1 mile from the A1. Burnmouth is the first village you pass through; Coldingham and St Abbs are just 5 minutes' drive beyond Eyemouth.

Travelling south from Edinburgh along the A1, take the coastal road, the A1107, just south of the ring road at Cockburnspath. The first village is Coldingham; from there branch left for St Abbs or right for Eyemouth.

Local police stations (Berwick: 01289 307111; Eyemouth: 01890 750217) are always able to give advice on road and traffic conditions, as can the AA and RAC.

By rail There is a main-line railway station at Berwick-upon-Tweed with connections from all over Britain (for timetable information telephone 0345 484950). The fast service from London takes only 3¾hrs and there are taxi-bus and taxi services from the station to take you on to either Eyemouth or St Abbs. The local dive centres can also arrange for pick-up from the station.

By ferry The ferry from Bergen, the Orkneys and Shetland docks at Aberdeen, and services from Amsterdam, Hamburg and Bergen come to

Newcastle upon Tyne. Hull, about four hours' drive away, has crossings from Zeebrugge and Rotterdam. As with the air connections, you can complete your journey by rail or by road.

Where to stay

Although there are a number of suitable hotels in the area, which vary in price depending on the facilities they have, many divers stay in local guest houses as these can be excellent value for money. They are very much a tradition in Berwickshire and most offer good, home cooked food. There are also a number of static caravan sites, reasonably cheap if there are several people sharing but harder work. It is also possible to find combined packages of accommodation, diving, meals and boat hire. The following places on or near the marine reserve are recommended:

Chirnside Hall Hotel, Chirnside, Berwickshire TD11 3LD (tel. 01890 818219).

MOTORING SERVICES

AA 24-hour breakdown service: 0800 887766 (0345 887766 from mobile telephones)

Green Flag motoring assistance: 0800 400600

RAC 24-hour breakdown service: 0800 828282

Eyemouth Auto Centre, Industrial Estate, Eyemouth (tel. 01890 750554)

Eyemouth Filling Station, Industrial Estate, Eyemouth (tel. 01890 751147)

Fisher's Brae Garage, Fisher's Brae, Coldingham (tel. 01890 771259)

French's Garage, Market Square, Coldingham (tel. 01890 771283)

Hogarth Motors, Acredale, Eyemouth (tel. 01890 750770)

Kwik-Fit, Castlegate, Berwick-upon-Tweed (tel. 01289 307288)

Northburn Garage, High Street, Eyemouth (tel. 01890 750216)

Tyre Services, Tweedside, Berwick-upon-Tweed (tel. 01289 306661)

Eyemouth Holiday Park, Fort Road, Eyemouth, Berwickshire TD14 5ES (tel. 01890 751050; fax 01890 751462; email lawson@ oceaneye.demon.co.uk).

Farne Diving Services, Beadnell, Northumberland NE68 7UA (tel./fax 01665 720615).

King's Arms Hotel, Hide Hill, Berwick-upon-Tweed TD15 1EJ (tel. 01289 307454; fax 01289 308867).

The Lodge, 146 Main Street, Seahouses, Northumberland NE68 7UA (tel./fax 01665 720158).

Melville House, Eyemouth Road, Coldingham, Berwickshire TD14 5NH (tel./fax 01890 771231; e-mail melvilhous@aol.com).

The Rest, St Abbs Village, Coldingham, Berwickshire TD14 5PP (tel. 01890 771681). Self-catering flat, sleeps 4.

Scoutscroft Holiday Centre, Coldingham, Berwickshire TD14 5NB (tel. 01890 771338; fax 01890 771746; e-mail scoutscroft@ compuserve.com).

The Ship Hotel, Harbour Road, Eyemouth, Berwickshire TD14 5HT (tel. 01890 750224).

Springbank Cottage, St Abbs Harbour, Berwickshire (tel. 01890 771477; fax 01890 771577).

St Abbs Haven Hotel, Coldingham Sands, Coldingham, Berwickshire TD14 5NZ (tel. 01890 771491).

Wheatsheaf Hotel, Main Street, Reston, Berwickshire TD14 5JS (tel. 01890 761219).

For a more comprehensive list of accommodation in the area, contact the Scottish Tourist Board at 23 Ravelston Terrace, Edinburgh EH4 (tel. 0131 332 2433; fax 0131 343 1513). They offer a superb service, will put you in touch with the other regional offices, and will make hotel bookings.

Places to eat

Most divers visiting the area tend to stay in self-catering or bed-and-breakfast accommodation. For those who are self-catering, there is a large Safeway supermarket at the A1 junction at Berwick-upon-Tweed and a Walter Wilson supermarket in Eyemouth. All the towns have small food shops, fish and chip shops, Chinese take-aways and pubs.

The following places to eat out are recommended:

Chirnside Hall Hotel, Chirnside, Berwickshire TD11 3LD (tel. 01890 818219). Excellent food and service. Award-winning restaurant, must dress accordingly.

The Coffee Shop, Northfield, St Abbs, Berwickshire (tel. 01890 771707). Home baking, great lunches between dives.

Foxtons, Hide Hill, Berwick-upon-Tweed TD15 1AB (tel. 01289 303939). Restaurant and wine bar, daily specials. Gets busy, so book a table. Casual/smart.

Magna Tandoori Restaurant, 39 Bridge Street, Berwick-upon-Tweed (tel. 01289 302736). Excellent Indian food, casual dress, large parties catered for.

Marshall Meadows Country House, on A1 between Eyemouth and Berwick (tel. 01289 331133). Great food, Sunday specials and Thursday buffet. Smart dress.

The Old Bakehouse, 4 Manse Road, Eyemouth, Berwickshire TD14 5JE (tel. 01890 750265). Licensed bistro, superb home cooking, parties catered for. Award-winning restaurant, casual dress.

Royal Garden Chinese Restaurant, 35 Maygate, Berwick-upon-Tweed (tel. 01289 331411). Great menus for large groups, reasonably priced, casual dress.

Other sources of information are: Eyemouth Tourist Information Centre, Auld Kirk, Market Place, Eyemouth, Berwickshire TD14 (tel. 01890 750678; Easter to October), the Scottish Borders Tourist Board, Municipal Buildings, 70 High Street, Selkirk (tel. 01750 20555; fax 01750 21886) and Berwick-upon-Tweed Tourist Information Centre, Castlegate Car Park, Berwick-upon-Tweed TD15 (tel. 01289 330733; fax 01289 330448).

Places to visit

The St Abbs Head Wildlife Reserve is a National Trust for Scotland and Scottish Wildlife Trust reserve covering some 190 acres, with a complex coastline and cliffs reaching over 90m. The National Trust for Scotland bought St Abbs Head in 1980 and it is considered the most important land-based seabird breeding colony on mainland Scotland. The most recent census showed over 80,000 breeding seabirds, primarily guillemots, razorbills, kittewakes, herring gulls, shags and fulmars. The reserve has been recognised as an important natural history location since the end of the 18th century.

Apart from seabirds, at least another 30 different species nest within the reserve and the central man-made loch, the Mire Loch. This sheltered valley also has several reptiles and a few species of butterfly that are regarded as nationally important. Over 300 different flowering plants have been found, as well as 40 lichens, 53 mosses and 9 liverworts.

Archaeologically, there are two specific areas of importance – the remains of an ecclesiastical building at Kirk Hill and monastic ruins at Nunnery Point. These date back to the time of St Ebba, and there have been several important excavations that have yielded particularly interesting finds, such as late Bronze Age ring-shaped armlets made of gold.

The reserve can be entered from its southern limit near St Abbs (NT 917 676) or by the lighthouse road, which forks off the B6438 Coldingham to St Abbs road at Northfield Farm (NT 913 674), where the wildlife reserve has a small display area next to the highly recommended tea room. Additional information on the St Abbs Wildlife Reserve can be obtained from the ranger, at Rangers Cottage, Northfield Farm, St Abbs (tel./fax 01890 771443).

There are also a number of national nature reserves well within reach – these as well as historic homes and castles are always a delight and well worth a visit. Particular points of interest are the Farne Islands, St Abbs Head, the Bass Rock, Floors Castle, Manderston and Paxton House. Information can be obtained from:

Association of Scottish Visitor Attractions, 4 Rothesay Terrace, Edinburgh EH3 (tel. 0131 555 2551; fax 0131 555 2552).

National Trust for Scotland, 5 Charlotte Square, Edinburgh (tel. 0131 226 5922; fax 0131 243 9302).

Scottish Battlefield and Historic Tours, 28 North Bridge, Edinburgh (tel. 0131 226 2202; fax 0131 226 2818).

Scottish Natural Heritage, Battleby, Redgorton, Perthshire PH1 3EW (tel. 01738 627921; fax 01738 630583).

Scottish Wildlife Trust, Cramond House, Cramond Glebe Road, Edinburgh EH4 6NS (tel. 0131 312 7765; fax 0131 312 8705).

OTHER PLACES TO VISIT

Eyemouth Museum, Manse Road, Eyemouth (tel. 01890 750678)

Fred Watson Studio, Northfield, St Abbs (tel. 01890 771588)

John Woods Gallery, Fisher's Brae, Coldingham (tel. 01890 771259)

National Trust for Scotland Visitor Centre, Northfield, St Abbs

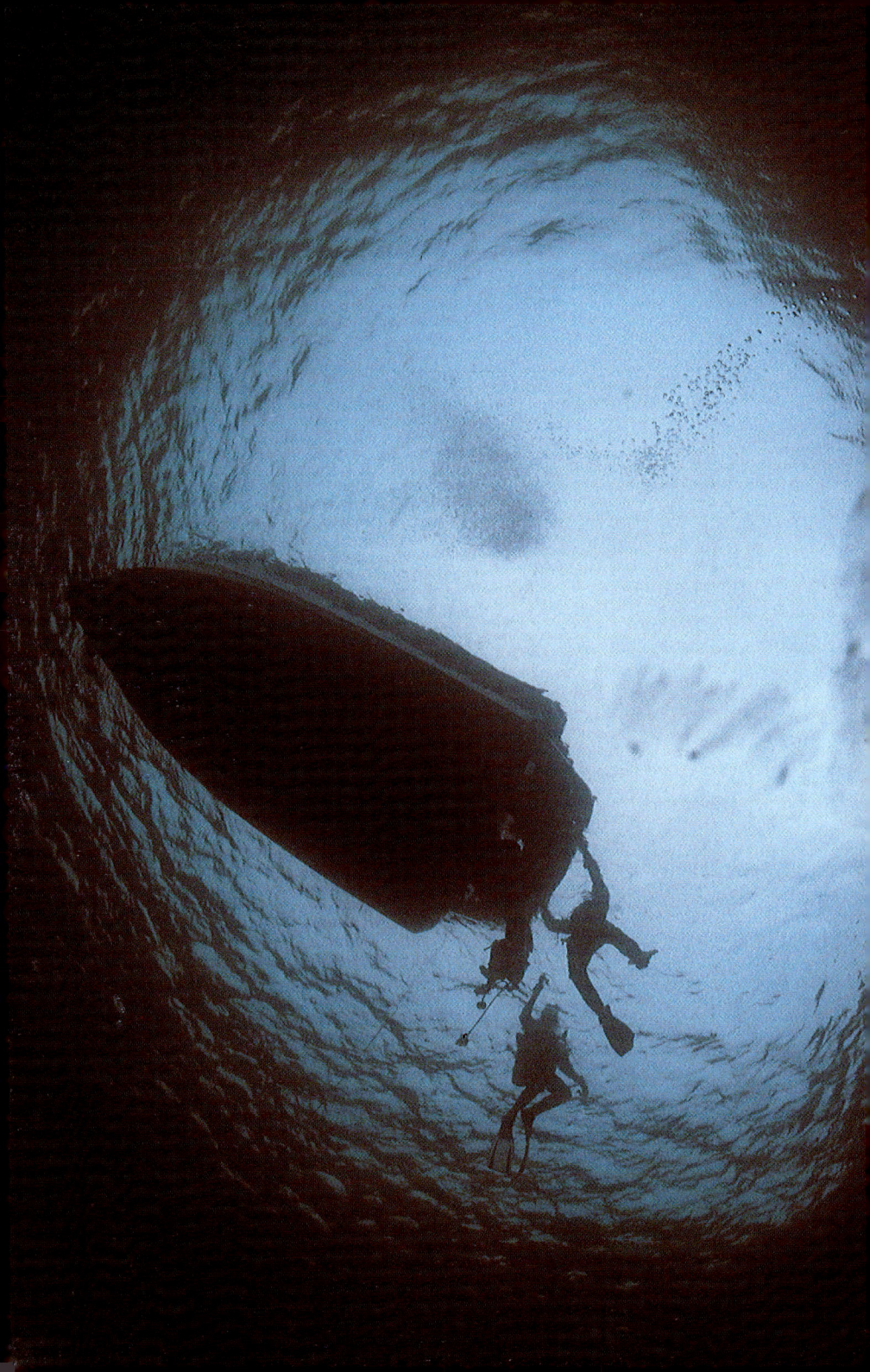

DIVE PLANNING

Ask almost any diver in Great Britain to name their favourite dive site or the name of the area they are planning to visit next and the names of St Abbs and Eyemouth will crop up over and over again. These unassuming little towns have earned a reputation in the diving world for being some of the best dive sites on mainland Britain for wealth and diversity of marine life. Those of you who do not agree with this unpretentious statement obviously have not experienced all that the Berwickshire coastline has to offer. The reasons are all too obvious when you get there!

Diver and site classification

It is never easy to recommend a system for classifying diver expertise or grading dive sites. Different conditions can be experienced on every dive – not to mention the possibility of rising currents or changeable weather. Divers' skills are only as good as their instructor's examiner and will vary depending on how often they are practised. In this book a typical American PADI style of diver classification has been adopted. It appears to work well in any part of the world:

Beginner New diver with a minimum of skill (fewer than 20 dives).

Intermediate Qualified diver, with a wider range of skill (fewer than 100 dives).

Advanced Experienced diver under all conditions.

The site grading is kept to four levels:

1 Easy dive close to shore access point; good snorkelling; can be some current.

2 Shallow dive (less than 15m) near shore or by boat, with some current to be expected.

3 Deeper dive; no decompression stops; current to be expected.

4 Deep dive, possibly including decompression stops; generally current.

Quite often the shallowest and easiest dive sites yield the highest rewards for marine life and sheer enjoyment. Being able to stay under longer in shallow water is by far the preferred diving method within the Marine Reserve, but there are more challenging dives for those who do not mind the time penalties that this type of diving imposes.

Wind and water conditions

The prevailing weather pattern is from the north-east, and many divers have travelled to St Abbs and Eyemouth only to find that they cannot get into the water. Please do not be put off – these northerly swells rarely last any length of time.

Water visibility alters drastically along the east coast of Scotland. The two main rivers in the area are the River Tweed at Berwick-upon-Tweed, 2 miles south of the Scottish border, and the River Eye at Eyemouth. During heavy, prolonged rainfall in the Borders, a large amount of muddy water is swept into the sea and may linger there for a few days. There have been several reports on the reduced visibility within the Marine Reserve area, following research by several qualified bodies, including the East of Scotland Water Authority, the Scottish Environmental Protection Agency, the Tweed River Purification Board and Herriot Watt University. It has been discovered that the greatest threat to visibility in the area comes from the Firth of Forth to the north. This massive estuary has been found to be the primary source of sedimentation along the entire south-east coast of Scotland.

There are no strong northerly tidal streams – the predominant direction of the tidal stream is south, except off the more exposed corner of St Abbs Head. Sedimentation therefore occurs after a prolonged onshore wind from the North Sea, bringing south the sediments from the Firth of Forth. Unfortunately, these onshore winds can also result in the entire east coast being too rough and dangerous for any type of diving. The average underwater visibility is around 6m, but 15m is the norm when offshore winds are experienced.

Very rough seas are generally short lived, particularly from March to October when the prevailing wind shifts to a westerly direction, which settles the sediment and brings flat, calm seas close to shore, even during the strongest of winds. When this is the case shore diving is recommended, as small diving boats such as inflatables or RIBs may well be blown off station. There are three times of the year that are particularly susceptible to violent, hurricane-force winds. These are

Divers at sunset, Pettico Wick.

during March, September and October. If you go back through historical records of ships being wrecked along the coast, almost all were wrecked during these months.

Although a few freshwater sites are mentioned in this guide they are generally used just as a "change", or perhaps for training. When the northerly storms do blow the only option for divers is to travel for 2½hrs to the closest sea loch on the west coast, Loch Long. Another half-hour's drive will take you to Loch Fyne – these sea lochs have sheltered, very deep water all year round, but sadly neither has an air station.

The outer reefs are more susceptible to offshore winds and, of course, the might of the North Sea swell and tidal range. Visibility here is always better and the water invariably has that blue quality. Tidal variations and current can be punishing to say the least, particularly off St Abbs Head, the Ebb Carrs and Hurker Rock, when converging currents reach over 4 knots running from opposite directions and meet over a connecting submarine ridge that rises from 35m to just 7m. Slack water is only 10 minutes during spring tides, but generally around 3hrs after high and low tide.

15

Weather forecasts

Marine Call offer a recorded information for all inshore areas (tel. 0891 500452; fax 0336 400452 for the east coast of Scotland).

The shipping forecast areas that lie on the south-east coast of Scotland are Forth and Tyne. Sea areas Dogger, Forties and Fisher lie to the east of Forth and Tyne and weather reports for these areas give an indication of future weather conditions on the east coast in a westerly tracking weather system.

An inshore shipping weather forecast is made on Radio 4 long wave (2,000KHz) at 5.55am, 1.55pm, 5.50pm and 12.48am. Forecasts are also broadcast on Radio 3 FM (90.2 to 92.4MHz): Monday to Friday at 6.55am, Saturday and Sunday at 7.55am. Gale warnings – winds forecast to be above Force 8 – are broadcast briefly at the end of all daytime news bulletins on Radio 4, as well as at the junction between programmes immediately following receipt. The weather forecast is also transmitted by the Forth Coastguard on Channel 67 at 2.05am local time and subsequently every four hours and by the Tyne-Tees Coastguard on Channel 67 at 1.50am and then every four hours, unless there is an emergency and all time and airwaves are in use. Those using a shipping radio should listen on Channel 16 and then switch to Channel 67 for the broadcast.

The local radio station, Radio Borders, gives hourly updates on road conditions throughout the area. Tune to FM 97.5 or 103.4MHz.

St Abbs Head.

23	dive site	∪∪∪	rocks and cliffs
7	depth in metres	||///	grassy slope
⌐⌐	mean low water springs	⌐ ⌐	footpath
∿	mean high water springs		buildings

Key to symbols used on dive site maps.

Tides

Further information on water movements can be gleaned from the Admiralty Tidal Stream Atlas or by contacting the local Coastguard. They are always willing to help – remember, they are not solely for emergency use.

The mean sea temperatures are 7.5°C in February, 9°C in May, 18°C in August and 10.5°C in November. Visiting divers should therefore make certain that they have proper thermal semi-dry or dry suits. Wind chill must also be considered. A good quality wet suit may be ideal underwater, but wind chill after leaving the water is commonplace – hypothermia can result from a long boat journey in cold, wet gear.

Tide times are taken from Leith. The tidal variation at Eyemouth is high water Leith minus 20 minutes; low water Leith minus 10 minutes. All tide times are quoted in GMT. Local tide tables are posted at the harbourmaster's office and Coastguard notice board in Eyemouth.

Dive flags and lights

The most-used flag in British waters is the International Code "A" flag. This consists of a white rectangular box on the inside and a blue box on the outside with an inverted "v" shape cut out of it. The other flag is the "divers down" flag, consisting of a red flag with a white diagonal stripe running top left to bottom right. It is an offence to show such flags if diving is not in progress. It is also an offence not to show the flag when diving is in progress.

"Divers down" lights are used when divers are diving at night. They are a series of three lights, red over white over red, displayed vertically, with a 360° visibility at a maximum of 200m. It is an offence to show such lights if diving is not in progress.

Contacting the Coastguard

The non-emergency telephone numbers for the Coastguard – to obtain information on sea and weather conditions or to report intended journeys and expeditions – are as follows:
Eyemouth: 01890 750348
Forth: 01333 450666
Tyne-Tees: 01912 572691
In emergency, dial 999 and ask for the Coastguard.

Diving emergencies and decompression illness

In the event of any possibly life threatening or serious diving incident, such as a diver lost or missing, or decompression illness or embolism, the Coastguard *must* be contacted direct and immediately. For a serious diving-related incident all other time-absorbing procedures will be overridden and that helicopter will be on its way to you in minutes.

Always call the Coastguard first. Whether onshore or at sea, contact the Coastguard direct on VHF Channel 16, or by dialling 999 and asking for the Coastguard.

Decompression illness symptoms vary between those so sudden that immediate air evacuation to a chamber is vital to those that might not become apparent for some hours. Some of these less dramatic symptoms, which may well be delayed, can be more serious and produce greater disability than the excruciating pain associated with a joint bend. Tingling and numbness are included in this category.

Air embolism or severe decompression illness symptoms require prompt but careful transfer of the subject to a recompression chamber. The victim should be laid flat on their back and, if possible, should be given 100% oxygen. If at sea, contact the Coastguard for help immediately: in a small boat, any attempt at speed may bounce the victim and almost certainly worsen the symptoms rather than help the situation.

If less dramatic symptoms of decompression illness occur inland, a GP or hospital casualty department (or the Coastguard) should be contacted. Emergency transfer to the nearest available recompression chamber will be arranged for you if it is necessary. Make sure you carry the following telephone numbers:
Aberdeen Royal Infirmary: 01224 681818 – ask for the duty diving doctor
Aberdeen Marine Laboratory: tel. 01224 876544

DOCTORS AND PHARMACISTS

Berwick Infirmary, Well Close Square, Berwick-upon-Tweed (tel. 01289 307484)

Boots the Chemists, Marygate, Berwick-upon-Tweed (tel. 01289 306036)

Caine Chemist, Church Street, Eyemouth (tel. 01890 750374)

Eyemouth Dental Practice, Houndlaw, Eyemouth (tel. 01890 750519)

Eyemouth Health Centre, Albert Road, Eyemouth (tel. 01890 750599)

G.C. Grey Pharmacy, Marygate, Berwick-upon-Tweed (tel. 01289 307387)

Fort William Underwater Training Centre: tel. 01397 703786

Glasgow Western Infirmary: tel. 0141 339 8822 – ask for the intensive care unit

Royal Victoria Infirmary, Newcastle upon Tyne: tel. 0191 232 5131 ext 24371.

The Military Remains Act

The Military Remains Act 1986 may in the future affect the wreck diver much more than it does at present. Its main drive is to preserve the sanctity of "war graves" – the wreckage of military ships and aircraft known to contain remains of service personnel.

The wreckage of all military aircraft of any nation is automatically protected, but ships will have to be designated by the Secretary of State and will need a statutory instrument to do so. This means that ships to be named as "war graves" will have to be named and approved by Parliament in the same way that ships to be protected as historic wrecks need a statutory instrument passed through Parliament.

There seems no doubt that those who passed the Act had little idea of the number of ships that could fall under its terms, such as a merchant ship with a Navy gunner aboard – was he among the survivors? – and as a result no ships have yet been named under the Act. This does not mean that ships are not covered by the general thrust of the Act and divers should therefore treat all possible "war graves" with total respect.

However, once these ships have been named, the diver commits an offence only by tampering with, damaging, moving, removing or unearthing remains, or by entering an enclosed interior space in the wreckage. The punishment on conviction of an offence is a fine. Nothing in the Act prevents the wreck diver from visiting the site, examining the exterior or even settling on the wreckage. An offence is committed only if the diver disturbs remains or enters a proper compartment of the wreck.

This is of course only a brief description, and serious wreck divers should study the Act itself. Your library or HM Stationery Office should be able to supply a copy.

The Merchant Shipping Acts

The Receiver of Wreck is responsible for the administration of the Merchant Shipping Act 1894 and the Merchant Shipping Act 1906, which deal with wreck and salvage. It is a legal requirement that all recovered wreck (flotsam, jetsam, derelict or lagan – whether recovered within or outside United Kingdom territorial waters) is reported to the Receiver of Wreck. The Coastguard act as the Receiver, and it is to them that recoveries should be reported.

Finders who conceal items are liable to prosecution, so any object – even if it appears to have no monetary value – should be declared as soon as possible. The Receiver of Wreck can then make a decision as to the future ownership of the property.

Wreck recovered from within United Kingdom territorial waters that remains unclaimed at the end of a statutory one-year period becomes the property of the Crown, and the Receiver of Wreck is required to dispose of it. This may be through sale at auction, although in many instances the finder will be allowed to keep unclaimed items of wreck in lieu of a salvage award. This, however, is at the discretion of the Receiver of Wreck, and each case is judged on its merits.

For further information contact: The Receiver of Wreck, The Coastguard Agency, Spring Place, 105 Commercial Road, Southampton SO15 1EG (tel. 01703 329474; fax 01703 329477).

The Protection of Wrecks Act

Divers who find a site that might be of historical, archaeological or artistic importance should leave everything as it is and report their findings, in confidence and as soon as possible, to the Department of National Heritage (or its equivalent in Northern Ireland, Scotland or

Wales). If appropriate, the wreck can then be designated under the Protection of Wrecks Act 1973, in order to control activities on the site.

Designated sites may only be dived or items recovered if a licence for that purpose has been granted; failure to comply with this is an offence and can result in a fine. All recoveries from designated sites must be reported to the Receiver of Wreck. For further information contact: The Secretariat of the Advisory Committee on Historic Wreck Sites, 3rd Floor, Department of National Heritage, 2/4 Cockspur Street, London SW1Y 5DH (tel. 0171 211 6367/8).

After the full moon in August and September you can find clumps of squid eggs amidst kelp fronds close to shore.

MARINE LIFE

Various different groups of plants and animals are to be found off the Berwickshire coast. As in many other parts of the world, local names for the same species can vary, so when identifying or describing a particular animal it is best to use its scientific name. The correct naming of a species is important for your own log-book, and is essential to scientists and marine biologists studying the flora and fauna now and in the future.

The PORIFERA, or sponges, are animals of so simple a structure that they are more like an aggregation or colony of protozoans. They are always attached and include such varieties as the purse sponge (*Scypha ciliata*) or *Myxilla incrustans*, perhaps the most common of all on the Berwickshire coast.

The COELENTERATA include a large number of relatively simple animals. There are two major groups: attached, like the anemones, and free swimming, like the jellyfish, one of the largest being the lion's mane jellyfish (*Cyanea lamarkii*). Many of the attached species are not solitary like the anemone, but consist of many united individuals like the hydroid *Tubularia indivisa*. The most common anemones found around St Abbs and Eyemouth are the plumose anemone (*Metridium senile*) and the dahlia anemone (*Urticina felina*); the latter has been chosen as the symbol of the Marine Reserve. Allied more closely to the anemones are the soft corals or ALCYONARIANS, such as dead men's fingers (*Alcyonium digitatum*), which consist of many individuals with a common skeleton of a horny substance, and the true corals, SCLERACTINA, such as the Devonshire cup coral (*Caryophyllia smithii*), which have calcareous skeletons.

The TURBELLARIA, or flat worms, are seldom more than 2.5cm long and are flat, transparent and sometimes parasitic. The NEMERTINA are soft-bodied worms that have a proboscis and are without the division of the body into transverse segments, such as the football jersey worm (*Tabulanus annulatus*).

The tunicates (TUNICATA) are exclusively marine and comprise many animals of different appearance. This group includes the sea squirts and

The Arctic anemone is common on deeper dives, always surrounded by brittlestars.

ascidians, such as the gooseberry sea squirt (*Dendrodoa grossularia*), and the light-bulb tunicate (*Clavelina lepadiformis*).

The ANNELIDA include the common lugworm (*Arenicola marina*), the segments of which are easily visible. POLYCHATE, or bristle worms, are exclusively marine and include the majority of marine worms. Many wander freely and are known as errant worms. Others, such as the peacock worm (*Sabella penicillus*) or sand mason worm (*Lanice conchilega*) are known as sedentary worms and always live in tubes of lime, sand or parchment-like material, which they make themselves and enlarge as they grow. Many types of worm have little in common with one another except their general shape.

POLYZOA are quite closely related to bristle worms. These are tiny creatures that always live in colonies and have a horny skeleton. The sea mat (*Membranipora membranacea*) is often found encrusting LAMINARIA or kelp species and seems to be the favourite diet of a number of sea slugs.

The ECHINODERMATA are a very diverse group that includes the starfish and the sea urchin. They are mostly slow moving, locomotion

24

Along for the ride – this hermit crab has the nudibranch *Limacea clavigera* living on its shell.

being performed by their peculiar tube-like feet through a "hydraulic" system supplied by canals throughout the body. They include five distinct groups – of the starfish or ASTEROIDEA, *Asterias rubens* is the most common inshore variety and *Ophiothrix fragilis* the most common of the brittlestar family, OPHIUROIDEA. Sea urchins, ECHINOIDEA, are found on all rocky ground and amidst kelp, the most common being *Echinus esculentus*, while sea cucumbers, HOLOTHUROIDEA, prefer the gravel sea beds of deeper water and you can often find large numbers of *Neopendactyla mixta*. Finally, there are the feather starfish (*Antedon bifida*) and sea lilies, CRINOIDEA, the most common on the Berwickshire coast off Burnmouth being *Antedon bifida*.

The ARTHROPODA comprise the largest number of species of any group in the animal kingdom. They have segmented bodies like the annelida, but have jointed limbs attached, which give the group their name. Of the four great divisions, three classes – insects, spiders and centipedes – are almost exclusively found on land, while the fourth, CRUSTACEA, is almost entirely marine. This last is such an all-embracing group that it includes water fleas, barnacles, sand hoppers, shrimps, prawns, lobsters, hermit crabs and many species of true crabs. Common species are the strident squat lobster (*Galathea strigosa*), the common spider crab (*Hyas araneus*), the common hermit crab (*Pagarus bernhardus*), the common prawn (*Pandalus montagui*) and the shore crab (*Cancer maenus*).

The MOLLUSCS form another group of considerable variety and include nudibranchs, chitons and octopus. Browsing on the kelp, the most common nudibranchs to be found are *Polycera quadrilineata* and *Dendronotus frondosus*. The GASTROPODA, or univalved shell fish, such as limpets, periwinkles and snails, usually have a one-piece shell and live mostly on the shore or sea bottom, but a few with greatly reduced shells swim near the surface. The most colourful of the shells is undoubtedly the painted topshell (*Calliostoma zizyphinum*). On rocky outcrops, European cowries (*Trivia monacha*) are common and necklace shells (*Natica catena*) can be found in sandy areas. BIVALVIA, bivalve molluscs, have a shell composed of more or less equal halves: of this group you can find queen scallops (*Aequipecten opercularis*) in the very deep waters off St Abbs Head; closer to shore, in sandy areas, razor shells (*Ensis siliqua*) are common. Another great division is the CEPHALOPODA, which includes squid, octopus and cuttlefish. Of the octopus, distinguished by their eight or ten tentacles or arms, the variety found most commonly in Scotland is the lesser octopus (*Eledone cirrhosa*). Off Eyemouth, the Atlantic cuttlefish (*Sepiola atlantica*) is a delight to find. A similar group is the BRACHIAPODA, often mistaken for molluscs.

Fish are divided into two principal groups: the ELASMOBRANCHS, which include dogfish, sharks and skate and have a relatively soft cartilaginous skeleton with the gill openings separate, such as the common dogfish (*Scyliorhinus canicula*); and TELEOSTS, or bony fish, which have hard bony skeletons and gill openings covered by flaps. The largest representatives of this family are the angler fish (*Lophius piscatorius*) and the wolf fish *(Anarhichas lupus)*.

A number of mammals have returned to the sea, usually living on or near the surface. Some are capable of diving to considerable depth, though they are always compelled to return to the surface for air. Within the CETACEA group are many kinds of whales, dolphins and porpoises; killer whales (*Orcinus orca*) are often seen cruising near St Abbs Head. Finally, there is the group PINNEPEDEA, which includes seals. Common seals (*Phoca vitulina*) can be found in quite large numbers north of Pettico Wick in early spring.

Above: The lesser octopus is quite common and changes colour rapidly when photographed. *Below:* A butterfish hiding in an empty mussell shell.

Plants

The sea is far poorer in terms of plant life than the land. Flowering plants have very few marine relatives, the best known being *Zostera*, or eel grass. The great majority of underwater plants are algae of a much simpler structure than flowering plants and produce spores rather than seeds. There are two main types of aquatic plant life: fixed and drifting.

Fixed marine plants can be split into three sub-groups, each of which has its own characteristic colour and structure. Green algae or CHLOROPHYCEAE, in which the chlorophyll is not masked by brown or red pigment, are generally of quite small size and simple structure. They include the sea lettuce (*Ulva lactuca*) and the long tubular fronds filled with air of *Enteromorpha intestinalis*. Brown algae or PHAEOPHYCEAE are the largest and sturdiest of all the algae and include the kelp plants also known as oarweed (*Laminaria digitata* and *Laminaria hyperborea*). On the foreshore, dabberlocks (*Alaria esculenta*) and the various wracks, such as the toothed wrack (*Fucus serratus*), bladder wrack (*Fucus vesiculosus*) and sea oak (*Halidrys siliquosa*) are common. Red algae or RHODOPHYCEAE are exclusively multicellular and generally of quite small size, the most common in Berwickshire being Irish moss or carragheen (*Chondrus crispus*), *Calliblepharis ciliata*, *Dilsea carnosa* and pepper dulse (*Laurencia pinnatifida*).

Kelp forests form a moving tangle of weed, which divers have to negotiate when diving from the shore.

Stinging cells

Anemones, corals and jellyfish are armed with a battery of stinging cells called nematocysts. These cells are tiny barbed harpoons tipped with a paralysing poison that the creature will fire into its prey should they happen to brush against it. These microscopic cells are particularly effective in the case of the lion's mane jellyfish (*Cyanae lamarkii*). Its tentacles can trail to a depth of over 6m and it is common during late spring and early summer, when large groups can be found in the water.

The seashore

The shore, where the sea meets the land, is primarily a dangerous and inhospitable place for any plant or creature. The cliffs are constantly being eroded by wind and rough seas, and strong tidal streams and brackish water (the combination of salt and fresh water) all present special problems to survival.

The extent to which the sea shore is uncovered depends on factors such as the lie of the land and the sharpness of the slope. There are essentially two types of shoreline, flat sandy bays and those formed of bedrock. Waves have the greatest influence in moulding the shore line. Often at spring tides all the sand is washed out and many rocks are uncovered for the first time in several seasons. Generally, the rocky shore does not alter much but the waves can gradually eat into the hard rocky coast – for example, under the Fort Point in Eyemouth a reasonably flat "abrasion" platform has been carved out, and in

---

SCIENTIFIC NAMES

In the scientific or binomial system for naming plants and animals, developed by Linnaeus and dating from the publication of his *Systema Naturae* in 1758, the first word is the genus to which it belongs, and always has a capital letter. This is followed by the specific or trivial name, which should not start with a capital. It is conventional to use italic type in publications, so *Cancer maenus*, for example, is the correct way to show the scientific name for the common shore crab. If a scientific name has three parts, the third describes a variant of the species, so *Sagartia elegans nivea* refers to the white form of the elegant anemone.

---

locations both south of Eyemouth at Hawk Ness and north of Pettico Wick there are a large number of sea caves that have been carved out of a softer substrate.

The monotonous regularity of the sea covering and uncovering twice daily and the ranges of temperature that vary so greatly, yearly if not daily, mean that it takes very hardy flora and fauna to stand up to these unrelenting conditions. It becomes obvious how hardy they are when you consider that ocean-going creatures can die in their millions at the slightest change of temperature or salinity in the water. Shore animals must adapt in many different ways for protection, feeding and, most important, reproduction. Yet in spite of the many difficulties the population of the sea shore is one of the densest and most varied habitats in the world. The effect of this density is the seemingly endless struggle of sea life to survive, whether by brute force, cunning or camouflage.

There are different sets of conditions under which the creatures live and yet we habitually find the same types of animal: worms, starfish, crustaceans and molluscs. All are adapted to the particular conditions under which they live. Some may be plant feeders and also live on the weed, others may browse on the algae-encrusted rocks, some burrow in the sand and some prey on the other species.

Rocky shores can be divided into zones or levels. Some types of shell occur at a higher level than others; there is a zone ruled by the barnacles that is, in turn, influenced by the amount of algae in the area and the other animals that live among the algae. The level of extreme low water is fringed by dense growths of large brown seaweeds. All levels are influenced by their degree of exposure and the zones are more readily marked out by their types of population than by their height. The zones can probably be best defined by the various species of weed to be found at the varying levels indicated earlier.

Marine conservation in Scotland

All the marine areas and coastline around Scotland come under the jurisdiction of Scottish Natural Heritage. Marine conservation is still in its infancy in the British Isles but there are many local groups and diving clubs affiliated to the Marine Conservation Society.

For information on local groups and expeditions, and how you can take part, please contact The Conservation Officer, Marine Conservation Society, 9 Gloucester Road, Ross-on-Wye HR9 5BU (tel. 01989 566017; fax 01989 567815).

MARINE RESERVE CODE OF PRACTICE

Safety

- Boat users must carry adequate equipment and ensure that someone reliable knows where they are going and when they will return.
- Divers must comply with safety requirements of the SSAC, BSAC, SAA, PADI, CMAS etc. Boats with divers down must fly the "A" flag.
- For advice and weather information contact HM Coastguard on 01333 450666.

Courtesy

- Maintain a high standard of behaviour and decency in public places.
- Obey parking regulations and park tidily, using bays where provided.
- Obey any special regulations which might apply, for example at harbours where the harbour master must be obeyed.

Conservation

- Fishing and sea angling by traditional methods are permitted, but obey fisheries regulations. Details from DAFS, Eyemouth Harbour Office (tel. 01890 750203). [*Author's note:* The Berwickshire coast is a Special Area of Conservation, and only registered fishing vessels will be allowed to operate. Collection of shellfish by divers will not be tolerated.]
- No spearguns, spears, hooks, gafs, etc, to be used underwater.
- Do not tamper with fishing gear or lobster pots (this is illegal and dangerous).
- Do not collect animals or plants within the Reserve.
- Do not leave litter, fishing line or chemicals (waste oil, paints etc.).
- Boat users, reduce speed close to cliffs at St Abbs Head to minimise disturbance to nesting sea-birds.
- Please remember that this is one of Britain's last wildernesses. Local people depend on it and thousands of visitors enjoy it and learn from it. Respect other users of the sea, and respect the wilderness.

The St Abbs and Eyemouth Voluntary Marine Nature Reserve

The Marine Reserve extends from Hurker Rock at Eyemouth to St Abbs Head and includes 4½ miles of coast, stretching out to the 50m depth contour. Since 1986 the Marine Reserve has been able to employ a warden, who has worked with divers, school groups, conservation organisations and local council authorities. Publicity material has been published and a code of conduct has been produced for visitors to the area. The Marine Reserve has seventeen member partners on its committee, including representatives of local authorities, diving clubs, the fishing community and conservation groups.

Continuing work within the Marine Reserve includes water temperature and clarity readings, marine life surveys and the maintenance of an important educational role. The European Union has recognised the significant part that the reserve has played in education and conservation, with the entire coastline being designated a Special Area of Conservation. This is still the only voluntary marine reserve in Scotland and has long been established as the ideal site for all standards of diver. In fact, those who are fortunate enough to dive here for the first time will never forget the experience.

Scottish Natural Heritage and the Marine Conservation Society both list the area as probably the best shore diving site in the entire British Isles. *BBC Wildlife Magazine* lists Killiedraughts Bay – within the reserve – as one of the top ten rock-pooling beaches in Britain. There is also a wildlife reserve at St Abbs Head (see page 10).

The full-time warden, who can be contacted on 01890 771273, is always on hand to give advice to visiting dive clubs on where to dive and what to expect to see.

Each week during the months of June to September there are organised rock pool rambles where you will be given an insight into some of the best rock pools in Britain. Weekly slide shows on conservation and the marine life within the reserve are particularly interesting. At the August Bank Holiday weekend the Marine Reserve hosts an annual underwater photography competition and slide show at St Abbs, which is excellent.

During the rest of the season there are educational projects within the local schools. A CD describing the marine life of the reserve – produced by the author, Neil Rutledge of Eyemouth Primary School, Fiona Crouch of the Marine Reserve, Scottish Borders Enterprise and Torness Nuclear Power Station – is now widely distributed within the schools and visitor centres in the area.

Looking out over Little Leeds Bay, with Hairy Ness Point to the right and St Abbs Head in the background.

BERWICK-UPON-TWEED TO EYEMOUTH

Berwick-upon-Tweed has a long and fascinating history, and a picturesque setting on the north bank of the River Tweed. Situated at the mouth of the river, on the border with Scotland, the walled town was always regarded as strategically important and reached the height of its prosperity during the reign of Alexander III (1247–86). Berwick was one of only four Royal Scottish Burghs and was compared in importance and size to Alexandria in the Lanercost Chronicle. In 1292 the English king, Edward I, granted Berwick in favour to John Baliol in the Great Hall of Berwick Castle, where eighty burghers of the town swore allegiance to Edward. When war broke out again in 1296 between the two kingdoms Berwick was the first to suffer and some historians claim that over 60,000 of the town's inhabitants were killed.

Owing to the prolonged impact of war on its economic growth, Berwick changed from being a thriving commercial and fishing sea port to an impoverished and insecure fortress town. In a treaty signed in 1502 it was regarded as an independent state "of", but not "within", the kingdom of England. It was not until 1836 that the town finally became a legal part of England. It now has a population of over 12,000 and is a very popular holiday destination. There is a new arts centre, the Maltings, and a new sports centre to the south of the river at Bonarsteads. Berwick-upon-Tweed is still very much a thriving market town, though, and the market takes place each Wednesday and Saturday throughout the year.

The inclusion of Berwick in this dive guide is to offer alternative freshwater sites, should the sea be too rough. There are a few other sites under bridges, at Coldstream, the Union Bridge, Norham and Kelso, all of which offer depths of over 6m. The stretch of coastline from Berwick to Burnmouth is the least dived area of all and has enormous potential, particularly off Burnmouth, where the rock strata run parallel to the shore, forming some superb offshore reefs with species of marine life

Opposite: Feather starfish are uncommon north of Eyemouth but are found in huge numbers off Burnmouth.

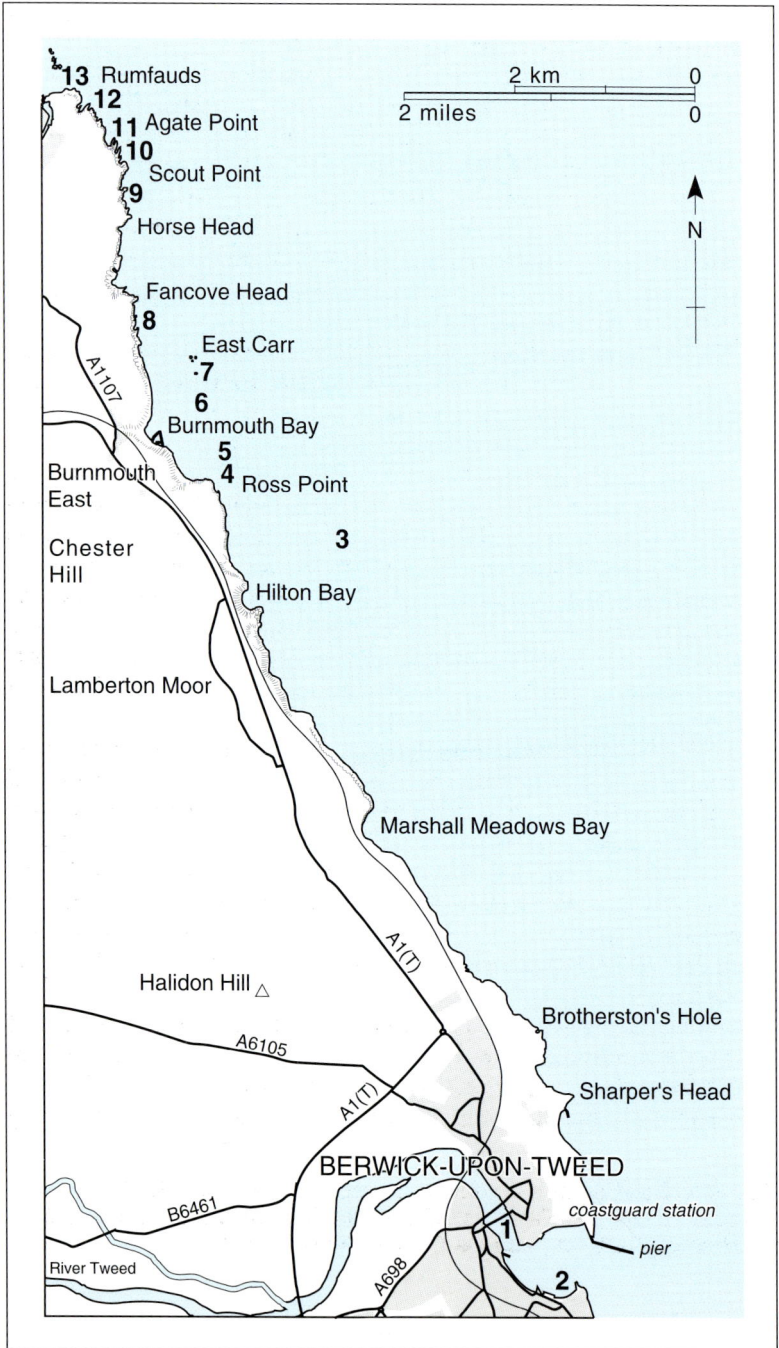

13 Rumfauds
12
11 Agate Point
10
9 Scout Point
Horse Head
Fancove Head
8
East Carr
7
6
Burnmouth Bay
5
4 Ross Point
3
Hilton Bay

Burnmouth East
Chester Hill
Lamberton Moor

Marshall Meadows Bay

Halidon Hill △

A6105

A1(T)

Brotherston's Hole

Sharper's Head

BERWICK-UPON-TWEED

coastguard station

1

pier

B6461

A698

2

River Tweed

A1107

2 km 0
2 miles 0

N

found nowhere else along the Berwickshire coast. The Berwick Harbourmaster may be contacted on 01289 307404.

BURNMOUTH has no beach and is built at the foot of a steeply inclined hill known locally as the "Brae". The shoreline is made up of a series of rocky ridges and reefs that run parallel to the shore and continue out beyond 30m. As the reefs extend underwater their shape alters until they resemble huge ripples of petrified sand, rising at an angle of 45° from the shore side for several metres and then dropping vertically on the offshore side. Wide sand gullies about 6m deep lie between these rocky ridges. The shallower reefs are all topped with kelp, the deeper offshore reefs with dead men's fingers.

The town of Burnmouth is split into four villages: Upper Burnmouth lies at the top of the hill; Ross, Cowdrait and Partanhall "doon the Brae". Burnmouth station was the terminus for the Eyemouth Railway, which was opened in 1891, but closed when the stopping service on the branch line was terminated in 1962. Although the station is no longer in use, the main line railway still passes through. Fishing from Burnmouth's rocky shore is primarily for lobsters and crabs. In fact, the name of one of the settlements – Partanhall – is derived from the word "parten", the local name for the common shore crab. A hard boat of the MFV type can be hired from Burnmouth harbour and there is also a rough shore entry slipway for launching boats. Storage of diving boats is not advisable, however, as Burnmouth harbour virtually dries up at low tide.

The most convenient way to dive the Burnmouth reefs is by launching from Eyemouth. Travelling time is only about 10 to 15 minutes by fast RIB and you will pass some of the geologically most important rock formations in the whole of Britain. There are layered folds of rock, forming many different convoluted shapes, and under the biggest cliff you will pass a series of three huge caves cut into the headland. The diving at Burnmouth is best done at half tide as both the South Carrs (Site **5**) and the Carr Rocks (Site **7**) are covered at high tide and difficult to find.

The town of EYEMOUTH was already a significant port by the time of its earliest mention in 1098, when King Edgar founded the priory at Coldingham. The monks from the priory retained land on the riverside in Eyemouth, or Emuth as was originally called, to facilitate the landing

Opposite: Berwick-upon-Tweed to Eyemouth (Sites 1 to 13). Wrecks in this area include the *Baron von Stjernbladt* (Site **3**), the *Congo* (Site **8**), the *President* (Site **10**) and the *Golden Sunset* (Site **12**).

Above: Burnmouth harbour with beach slipway.

Below: The new harbour at Eyemouth from the slipway.

and storage of their supplies. Eyemouth is still the largest town in Berwickshire.

The Treaty of Boulogne stipulated that its fort on the promontory overlooking the "Roadsteads", or Eyemouth Bay, had to be destroyed as it was seen to be a threat to the tenuous peace held between Scotland, England and France. James VI visited the town and declared Eyemouth a Burgh of Barony in 1597, with the added privilege of being a free port.

The Berwickshire coastal fishing villages still live under the shadow of the terrible disaster that hit the east coast on 14 October, 1881. "Black Friday", as it came to be known, saw the loss of 189 men during a sudden tempest. A constant reminder to this terror is the tapestry on permanent display in the Eyemouth Museum.

Eyemouth is a busy, thriving fishing port with a new harbour and a new sewage treatment plant, an 18-hole golf course, new housing and industrial developments and a holiday caravan park. There are two slipways that may be used, free of charge, for the launching of dive boats. The one inside the harbour and conveniently opposite a car park next to the Fisherman's Mutual Association can only be used from mid to high tide as the water drops off the end of the slipway to a set of steps, making it almost impossible to launch or retrieve craft. The other slipway is near the harbour entrance, opposite the Old Cobble House. This slipway runs onto the beach and may be used at any state of tide. It is by far the more popular as four-wheel drive vehicles are allowed onto the beach. Please be aware of other users of the beach, though.

1 Old Bridge

Overall Grade – 2. *Location* – Between the harbour wall and the first pier of the Old Bridge, Berwick-upon-Tweed, at 55 46 06N; 02 02 12W. *OS Grid Reference* – NU 997 528. *Average Depth* – 6m. *Typical Current Conditions* – Must be dived on incoming tide at high tide. *Expertise Required* – Intermediate. *Access* – From the shore at north-east side of bridge.

The northern and seaward side of the Old Bridge in Berwick is an excellent alternative when the sea is too rough. It is best dived on an incoming tide when the downward push of the river is offset against the flow of the incoming current, creating an element of slack water. It is best to dive this site nearer high tide. The walls of the old pier side are covered in mussels (*Mytilus edulus*) and you will find harbour crabs (*Carcinus maenus*), edible crabs (*Cancer pagarus*), flounders, blennies, gobies, butterfish (*Pholis gunnellus*) and numerous nudibranchs – which, interestingly, do not seem to be affected by the mixture of fresh and sea water. As you approach the piers supporting the bridge the walls are deeply undercut by the action of the river and there are always interesting finds to be made.

2 The Shad

Overall Grade – 2. *Location* – At bend of river opposite Berwick Yacht Club, at 55 46 12N; 01 59 42W. *OS Grid Reference* – NU 004 519. *Average Depth* – 5m. *Typical Current Conditions* – Can be strong, best to dive on incoming tide at mid-tide level. *Expertise Required* – Beginner (under supervision). *Access* – Shore dive at Spittal end of river mouth.

This bend near the mouth of the River Tweed is best dived at mid tide on an incoming flow, when you are still able to make out the angle of the deeper channel of the river. If you enter from the beach side opposite the Berwick Salmon Company and Berwick Yacht Club there is easy shore access. This site is located at the junction of the road where the twin towns to the south of the River Tweed, Tweedmouth and

The Shad on the River Tweed.

Spittal, merge. Both are generally classed as Berwick – unless you live there!

The river channel quickly slopes away and if you follow the current upstream you will come to an old dock with eroded and rotten wood and steel supports. The start of this dock is the best point of exit. The river bed has a profusion of life passing through it, including plaice (*Pleuronectes platessa*), pogge (*Agonus cataphractus*) and, if you are lucky, salmon.

It should be noted that the season for fishing salmon by traditional methods in the River Tweed is between 14 February and 14 September inclusive, and deference should always be made to this: if there are people fishing, do not dive! Otherwise, enjoy the site – it makes a great alternative to the sea and is ideal for training sessions.

3 Baron von Stjernbladt

Overall Grade – 4. *Location* – South-east of Ross Point, at 55 50 00N; 02 02 00W (position approximate). *Average Depth* – 30m. *Typical Current Conditions* – Variable to strong. *Expertise Required* – Advanced. *Access* – By boat only, from Eyemouth or Burnmouth.

This as yet undived wreck lies approximately south-east of Ross Point and has been the focus of searches for many years, including a serious attempt in 1996, which revealed only piles of stones and offshore submarine seamounts. A magnetometer would be essential to find this ship. The *Baron von Stjernbladt* was a Danish merchant ship that struck a mine on 23 April, 1917. The 991-ton ship caught fire and sank rapidly with much loss of life. The charted location is 53 50 00N; 02 02 00W in 25m of water, with a clearance of 15m. The author can assure readers, however, that the wreck is not at these co-ordinates.

The sea bed within the vicinity is largely made up of loose gravel and sand ridges that run into the continuing line of the reefs. On these rocky reefs, which are more common to Burnmouth, you can find feather starfish and, in the sand gullies, large concentrations of sea cucumbers, considered rare within the confines of the Marine Reserve.

4 Ross Point

Overall Grade – 2. *Location* – Opposite the first headland south of Burnmouth, at 55 50 24N; 02 03 18W. *OS Grid Reference* – NT 967 605. *Average Depth* – 12m. *Typical Current Conditions* – Slight. *Expertise Required* – Beginner. *Access* – By boat only, from Burnmouth

Leopard-spotted gobies can be found in most sandy caves and crevices and are a delightful photographic subject.

or Eyemouth.

The tumbled cliff and boulders that form the start of the reef from Ross Point merge into a reef that runs parallel to the shore and is called Brisset. This whole area is absolutely superb for marine life. On the more exposed sides of the reef can be found the sea oak algae, which grows in huge concentrations. Look closely among this curiously shaped algae with its knobbly bladders, which resemble the seed pods of its terrestrial counterpart. Here you will find butterfish, pipefish (*Sygnathus acus)* and hundreds of shrimps of several species, including chameleon shrimps (*Hippolyte inermis*) and longsnout shrimps (*Hippolyte longirostris).*

The vertical walls run for hundreds of metres and are always surrounded by schools of pollack (*Pollachius pollachius*) and saithe (*Pollachius virens*). Scorpion fish (*Taurulus bubalis*) are common, as are conger eels (*Conger conger)*, crabs, lobsters and squat lobsters. This site is also considered to be an easy drift dive when the tide is in flood.

5 South Carrs

Overall Grade – 3. *Location* – Directly out from Ross Point, at 55 50 30N; 02 03 18W. *OS Grid Reference* – NT 966 608. *Average Depth* – 12m. *Typical Current Conditions* – Variable. *Expertise Required* – Beginner. *Access* – By boat only, from Burnmouth or Eyemouth.

The South Carrs is a series of rocky pinnacles found at low tide. Topped with kelp, they are formed at the start of a very long submarine reef, which runs adjacent to the shore for several hundred metres, with few breaks in between. The wall rises approximately 9m and this is quite possibly one of the best wall dives along the Berwickshire coast.

The wall is rugged with many nooks and crannies, small caves, gullies and canyons and every section of rock is covered in dead men's fingers, various types of sponge, hydroids, tunicates, nudibranchs and squat lobsters. The strident squat lobster is particularly colourful, with its bright orange carapace painted with iridescent blue lines.

At the bottom of the wall can be found a jumble of stones, which is home to many families of ballan wrasse, goldsinny (*Centrolabrus rupestris*) and leopard-spotted gobies (*Thorogobius ephippiatus*). Flounders abound the gravel beds and the topknot (*Zeugopterus punctatus*) can be seen clinging to the underside of rocky ledges. Sun starfish (*Crossaster papposus*) are commonly found feeding on brittlestars and, in fact, there are at least ten species of starfish to be found along this wall. This whole area is well worth exploring and could easily be split up into many separate dives.

6 Ross Carrs

Overall Grade – 3. *Location* – Directly opposite Burnmouth harbour, at 55 50 42N; 02 03 19W. *OS Grid Reference* – NT 965 615. *Average Depth* – 18m. *Typical Current Conditions* – Variable. *Expertise Required* – Intermediate. *Access* – By boat only, closest to Burnmouth.

This dive is on the series of rocky reefs running parallel to the shore. Here, long low stands of rocky ridges have formed "waves" consisting of the rocky reef separated by sand patches. The sand and gravel patches are home to sea cucumbers, sea pens (*Virgularia mirabilis*), tunicates and the sea squirt *Molgula manhattensis*. Sand gobies (*Pomatoschistus minutus*) are everywhere, as are the much rarer black gobies (*Gobius niger*).

The ridges are covered in dead men's fingers and there are always butterfish, dragonets (*Callionymus lyra*) and wrasse. Large cod (*Gadus morhua*) patrol the upper part of the reef and prey on the smaller schools of pollack and saithe. Underwater visibility is generally good in this area and you can quite clearly see the other reefs running parallel, so it is easy to spread out over a wider area and explore sections of this incredibly scenic dive. This site should not be missed.

7 Carr Rocks

Overall Grade – 2. *Location* – To the east and north of Burnmouth harbour, at 55 51 00N; 02 03 42W. *OS Grid Reference* – NT 963 617. *Average Depth* – 12m. *Typical Current Conditions* – Variable. *Expertise Required* – Intermediate. *Access* – By boat only, closest point is Burnmouth harbour.

This set of rocks is at the northern edge of the strip reef running parallel to the shore from the South Carrs (Site **5**). The reef formations terminate around this jumble of house-sized boulders, split into two groups and known as East Carr and West Carr to local fishermen. These continue into the shore, where different rock strata commence and form massive cliffs of old red sandstone mixed with a conglomerate. The softer strata have been eroded away in certain points to form deeply cut ravines and long caves.

The huge rocky boulders that form the Carr Rocks are covered in three varieties of kelp, each of which delineates an underwater level of marine life. The mid-range kelp, which grows to a depth of 9m, is smothered in an algal fuzz called *Obelia geniculata*. This type of hydroid is the favourite food species for quite a number of

The squat lobster is the most colourful of all the crustaceans found on the reserve. Its vivid blue colours are picked out by divers' torches.

nudibranchs, including *Dendronotus frondosus*, *Eubranchus farrani* and *Coryphella pedata*. The upper layers of kelp are also smothered in the sea mat, a type of bryozoan called *Membranipora membranacea*, which is a flat expanding colony of thousands of tiny individual cells. These are the main food for two other species of nudibranch: *Limacea clavigera* is one of the most common of all to be found on the east coast and *Polycera quadrilineata* comes in a multitude of different colour variations.

The lower reaches of the boulders are home to soft corals, anemones, spider crabs, squat lobsters, starfish and shrimps. There are always fairly large schools of fish around these boulders and most will come quite close to you. Have a look at the sand and gravel patches near the base of the rocks because you will often find the delicate tubes of the sand mason worm sticking up from the sand.

8 Congo

Overall Grade – 2. *Location* – Opposite Gull Rock between Burnmouth and Eyemouth, at 55 51 18N; 02 04 12W. *OS Grid Reference* – NT 958 622. *Average Depth* – 9m. *Typical Current Conditions* – Slight, but can

Polycera quadrilineata is one of several nudibranchs commonly found along this coastline.

be surge close to shore. *Expertise Required* – Beginner. *Access* – By boat only, from either Eyemouth or Burnmouth.

The remains of the *Congo* lie scattered at the foot of Gull Rock, a single pinnacle standing alone to the north of Burnmouth harbour. This steamship struck the boulders near the Gull Rock in thick fog after suffering engine trouble. The ship was completely wrecked and only the scattered remains can be found. The propeller was salvaged but you can still see the old windlass. This wooden ship had a sheath of thin copper to ward off damage by ship worm and to provide extra strengthening. Strips of copper can still be found on the site, often wedged under boulders and amidst the kelp of the foreshore.

The location itself, surrounded by large boulders topped with kelp, is very interesting and provides a number of avenues for exploration. The sides of the rocks are fairly smooth and well encrusted with soft corals, sponges, anemones and hydroids. Ballan wrasse are common, as are pollack and saithe, with a few much larger cod also in evidence. Although seals are not common along the coast, being concentrated on the Farne Islands and the Bass Rock in the Forth, they have been seen along this stretch of coast, sunning themselves on the rocks, as it is accessible only from the sea and has no beach whatsoever.

9 Horse Cave, Dove Cave and Scout Cave

Overall Grade – 2. *Location* – The three caves bisecting the Hawkness headland, at 55 51 36N; 02 04 18W. *OS Grid Reference* – NT 956 634. *Average Depth* – 12m. *Typical Current Conditions* – Slight, but can be strong surge in the caves. *Expertise Required* – Beginner on calm days, otherwise Intermediate. *Access* – By boat only.

Travelling north from Burnmouth, Scout Cave is the first real cave to be spotted, cutting into the headland. On taking the boat around to the other side of the headland an even larger cave, Dove Cave, can be found. The two caves look as if they may connect underwater, or underground at least, but they have been explored by many people over the years and apparently do not. It was originally thought that Dove Cave may have linked into the now bricked-up underground passageways under the Gunsgreen mansion house in Eyemouth. These caves were supposedly used by smugglers during the 19th century.

Scout Cave is the least interesting of the two, in that it does not go as far into the headland as Dove Cave, but the walls are still covered in marine life, particularly small sea squirts, hydroids, anemones and algae. Scorpion fish are common, but particularly interesting around June and early July are juvenile cormorants and shags, which congregate at the mouth of the cave and will swim underwater with you when you approach them.

There is also what appears to be a false cave on the surface that "bells out" underwater and extends some 15m under the headland. Most divers miss this site because of the proximity and very obvious nature of the other caves. The undersea strata have also formed a dyke, which juts out from the headland and forms the north side of Horse Cave. Looking at the cave from the seaward side, it is only a shallow depression of about 3m, but underwater it suddenly falls away and a tunnel, carved by the relentless action of the waves, continues into the headland. The sides of the cave are worn smooth and covered in encrusting algae, hydroids and gooseberry sea squirts (*Dendrodoa grossularia*). The sea bed is made up of well-worn rounded stones and gradually makes way for a boulder bed coinciding with the underside of the main part of the cliff.

Dove Cave may be snorkelled all the way in, as there is an air space above you. In fact, at low tide you should also be able to take your boat quite far in as it is around 7m deep for most of the way. The sides and bottom of the cave are made of sandstone and have been carved smooth by the waves. Algae debris is usually present on the bottom, particularly during the spring and autumn plankton blooms, and huge concentrations of jellyfish may be swept into the cave, including the larger – and stinging – lion's mane jellyfish. The common starfish is particularly common here and can be found on almost every available surface, from the sides of the vertical walls to the sand and gravel.

10 President

Overall Grade – 2. *Location* – South of Agate Point, off Eyemouth at 55 55 21N; 02 04 30W. *OS Grid Reference* – NT 955 641. *Average Depth* – 9m. *Typical Current Conditions* – Slight, but can be surge. *Expertise Required* – Beginner. *Access* – Can be dived from the shore, but better by boat.

The *President*, built in 1907 and registered in Sunderland, ran aground during thick fog on 29 April, 1928 on a rocky reef known as Whup Ness. At the time she was travelling from Hamburg to Methil in Fife. Weighing 1,946 gross tons she stood little chance as she ploughed into the channel between the rocks and became wedged with her stern facing the shore, so tightly that the crew managed to climb ashore by means of

The *President*, aground on Whup Ness.

a ladder. Unfortunately, the weather conditions soon changed and the ship was completely destroyed.

The main boilers sit upright in a sandy gully in 12m and wreckage is scattered over a very wide range. While some of the larger plates are 20m deep, there is wreckage to be found in only 1m. The overlapping steel plates and girders have become firmly wedged under rocks and much of the algae, and even the crabs and lobsters, have taken on a rusty hue. Eyemouth and District SAC own the salvage rights for the ship, having discovered that the wreck was unclaimed and abandoned, and first dived her on 25 May, 1963. Over the years, after successive winter storms, the *President* has turned up many interesting artefacts, such as wide-bore copper piping, brass light fittings and portholes, all with glass intact and even in working condition.

11 The Cauldrons

Overall Grade – 2. *Location* – At Agate Point, the headland to the north of the *President* wreck, at 55 52 24N; 02 04 34W. *OS Grid Reference* – NT 954 644. *Average Depth* – 15m. *Typical Current Conditions* – Variable, particularly on the headland, and can be surge inshore at the Cauldrons. *Expertise Required* – Intermediate. *Access* – By shore, difficult climb after a long walk, better by boat from Eyemouth.

This is another one of those dual dive sites that could be dived in many different combinations, but is more generally done at one time. The Cauldrons form the inshore part of a narrow gully that runs directly into the grassy headland. Owing to the geology of the rock some of it has been carved out by the sea, creating huge pot-shaped holes or cauldrons. The largest of these is entered through a narrow hole at the base and is circular inside, owing to the whirlpool action created by the waves and small stones. Encrusting sponges, chiton shells and beadlet anemones (*Actinia equina*) are common here.

The gully is very narrow and, being quite close to the Eyemouth Golf Course, contains numerous golf balls. As you continue out to sea along the reef, follow the wall on your right – you will eventually come to the end of this reef, but continue seaward and pick up the next one. It is here that you will find an underwater archway that rivals Cathedral Rock (Site **29**). It is covered in soft corals, anemones, blennies, gobies and some very large cod.

Butterfish are common, as are dragonets, short-spined scorpion fish (*Myoxocephalus scorpius*) and lumpsuckers (*Cyclopterus lumpus*) during the spring breeding season. On the other side of the archway the bottom is sand and gravel where flounders and sand gobies can be found. Offshore you will come across another long strip reef, which is also superb for exploring. It is best to be picked up by the boat cover at this point.

The short-spined scorpion fish is the most common of the scorpion fish and has a voracious appetite.

12 Golden Sunset

Overall Grade – 2. *Location* – Off "Polly", a group of large rocks isolated from the shore by narrow gullies, at 55 52 30N; 02 04 36W. *OS Grid Reference* – NT 953 646. *Average Depth* – 9m. *Typical Current Conditions* – Slight, but can be surge inshore. *Expertise Required* – Beginner. *Access* – By boat from Eyemouth.

The *Golden Sunset* was a motor fishing vessel that struck the rocks, caught fire and sank on the way to Eyemouth harbour during a severe storm. Wedged between the biggest of the gullies and the little pinnacle, and being a wooden boat, she soon succumbed to the ravages of the weather and very little of her remains. The engine block is still there, but the propeller was salvaged by Eyemouth and District SAC many years ago.

Among the rocky pinnacles and gullies are many interesting routes. This is an ideal area for training when the sea is calm and is superb for photography, with its vertical walls covered in soft corals, anemones and sponges. The whole of this stretch of rocky coastline has reefs, gullies and rocks, which run at 45° to the shore and aim towards Hurker Rock and on towards St Abbs, making for some leisurely exploration while you cross from one gully to the next. This is a superb diving site for photography. It is above these rocks and the next gully, called Rumfauds, that the new marine interpretive centre is to be situated.

13 Greenends Gully

Overall Grade – 1. *Location* – Just before the headland that becomes Rumfauds, at 55 52 32N; 02 04 54W. *OS Grid Reference* – NT 949 647. *Average Depth* – 7m. *Typical Current Conditions* – Nil in the gully, but can be strong on the exposed headland. *Expertise Required* – Beginner. *Access* – From the shore or by boat.

Greenends Gully has always been a favourite with divers as it has easy, sheltered access, often during the worst of weather conditions. From the shore, the gully angles out towards Hurker Rock (Site **14**) and comes to a "Y" junction. The left-hand wall is vertical and in some places deeply undercut by ledges where squat lobsters and octopus lurk. If you travel to the right at the junction you will come across a rise of smooth stones – follow a narrow gully up to the right through the headland and this will bring you to the start of Rumfauds.

When you take the left-hand junction you will come across another rise piled high with smooth stones. Follow the reef to your left and you will eventually come to a series of narrow gullies that will take you into a sheltered bay behind the reef of Dulse Craig. This is now part of the new harbour development, but the offshore reefs run like "fingers" and there is huge potential for exploration.

Greenends Gully, Eyemouth.

BAREFOOTS MARINE RESERVE

Only the first six dives in this section of the coast are within the Barefoots Marine Reserve; the remaining six sites lie along the coast to the north-west or offshore. Many divers say that these dives are preferred to the shore dives at St Abbs, because of the ease of access and ample parking.

Little Leeds Bay (Site **18**) used to suffer greatly from a nearby sewage outfall, but thankfully East of Scotland Water are, at the time of writing, constructing a new sewage treatment plant to the south of Eyemouth. The only outfall through the old pipe may be biodegradable vegetable matter from a nearby factory for a few weeks of the year, though it will also be used as a storm water run-off.

The main area of the dive sites is privately owned by Eyemouth Holiday Park, and permission to dive must be obtained from reception. There is a fee for parking, but this pays for the upkeep of the steps, as well as free use of showers and toilets. Divers are welcome at this site and there is ample space for everyone. Traditional sea angling is also allowed off the rocky headlands, so divers should be aware of this and the possibility of becoming entangled in fishing line. Divers are encouraged to remove any line, weights or hooks that have become entangled on the rocky substrate or kelp.

14 Hurker Rock

Overall Grade – 3. *Location* – Opposite Eyemouth Bay, acting as a natural breakwater at 55 52 40N; 02 05 00W. *OS Grid Reference* – NT 948 649. *Average Depth* – 15m. *Typical Current Conditions* – Variable to strong, possible surge on outside. *Expertise Required* – Intermediate. *Access* – By boat only.

Hurker Rock is the largest of the hard rocky promontories that form the natural breakwater protecting Eyemouth Bay. The sides of the rock are

Opposite: Diver in Weasel Loch.

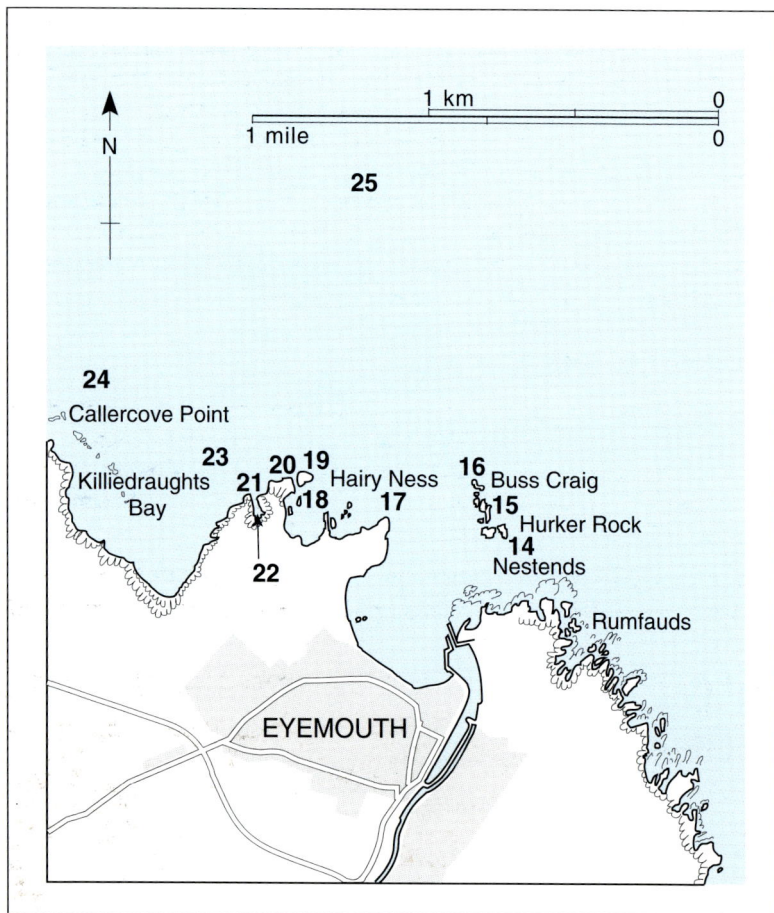

Barefoots Marine Reserve (Sites **14** to **25**). Wrecks in this area include the *Mauretana* (Site **16**) and the *Spes-Bona* (Site **17**).

steeply sloped and fringed in kelp. Beneath the kelp line at 8m depth, soft corals, anemones and sponges grow in great profusion. There are numerous ledges with squat lobsters and leopard-spotted gobies. Hermit crabs are everywhere and at the bottom of the rock a low reef extends its fingers out into deeper water.

This low reef is covered in dead men's fingers, brittle stars and sun starfish, which feed on the more fragile brittlestars. The seven-armed starfish (*Luidia ciliaris*), the largest of all the east-coast starfish, is also found here. This is an active predator on the sea bed and will attack molluscs, heart urchins (*Echinocardium cordatum*) and other starfish. This whole reef is swept by current, so only low encrusting life is found here. However, there are many interesting nudibranchs, shells and crustaceans. If you follow Hurker Rock around to the north and west, you will come to a narrow vertical-walled canyon, which twists its way through to the sheltered bay on the other side. Wolf fish are always found here, generally in mating pairs, the female being brown in colour as opposed to the grey male.

15 Hincar Rock

Overall Grade – 3. *Location* – Opposite Eyemouth Bay, acts as a natural breakwater, at 55 52 42N; 02 05 03W. *OS Grid Reference* – NT 947 650. *Average Depth* – 15m. *Typical Depth* – 15m. *Typical Current Conditions* – Variable to strong, possible surge on outside. *Expertise Required* – Intermediate. *Access* – By boat only.

Hincar Rock is visible at high tide, but sometimes by as little as 1m when the spring tides are especially high, particularly during the spring and

Sun starfish are active predators, feeding on the more fragile brittlestars.

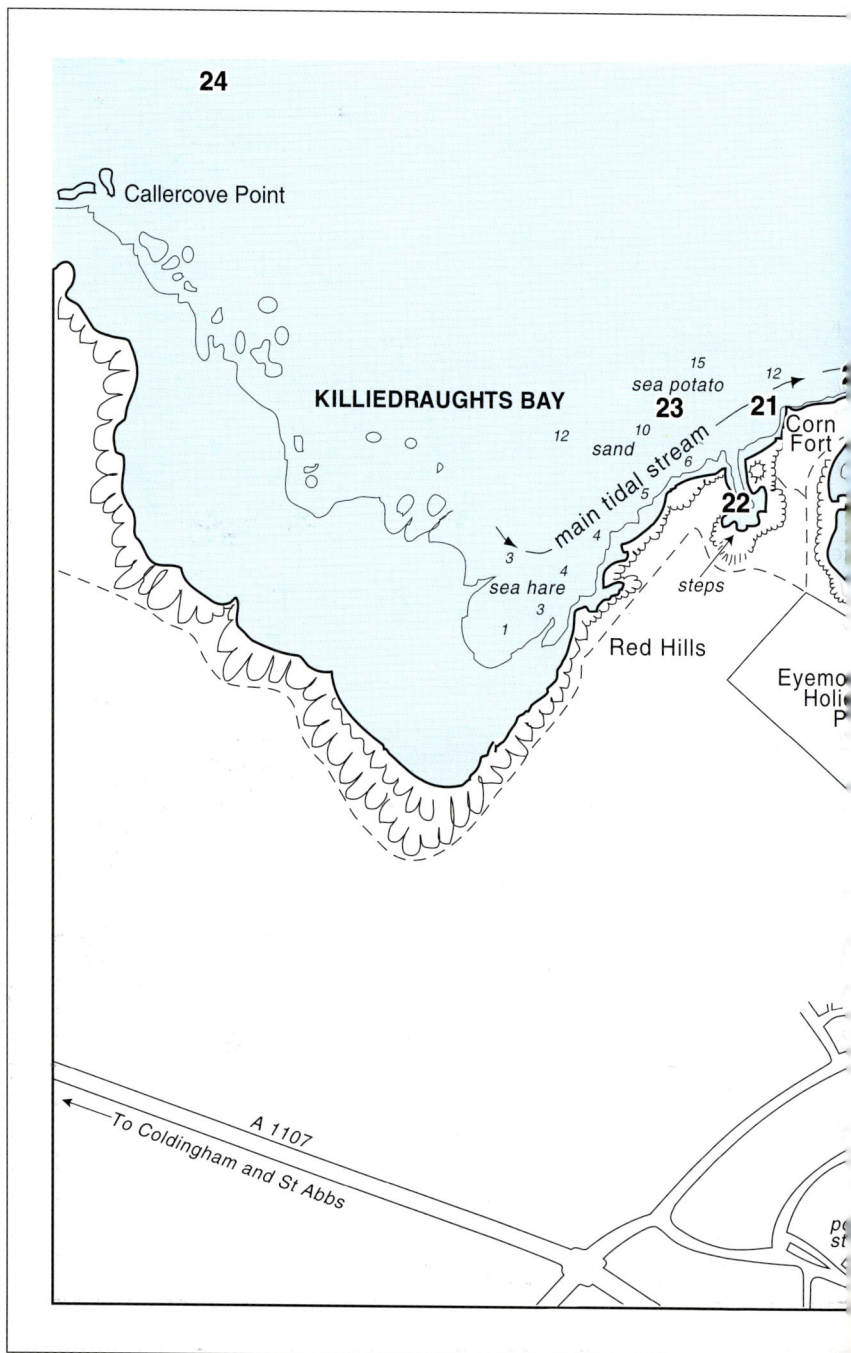

24

Callercove Point

KILLIEDRAUGHTS BAY

15
sea potato

23   **21**

12   *sand*   10   Corn
5   6   Fort

main tidal stream

3   4
4
sea hare   3

22

1   steps

Red Hills

Eyemo
Holi
P

A 1107
To Coldingham and St Abbs

p
st

200 m   0

200 yds   0

Ness

16

...ibranchs

11 big fish

12

26 spiny spider crabs

16 20

Buss Craig

11 nudibranchs

12 seals

15

Luff Hard Reef

big fish (very picturesque)

17

8

10

15

18

22

4 3

12

9

Hincar Rock

Sunstars

12

20

5

8

14 16

...eeds

large rocks

10

Hurker Briggs Rock

Black Carr

8 9

9

Fort

7

EYEMOUTH BAY

15

kelp

squat lobsters

Nestends

13 arch

11 11

...stguard ...on

8

5

12

9 11

9

11

14

sand

7

2 2 4

0

2

1 1

Tam Stone

0°

Green Ends

Rumfauds

...ming pool

beach

slipway

golf course

car park

slipway

garage

phone box

N

...YEMOUTH

lifeboat

phone box

gate

health centre

harbour slipway

autumn equinoxes. It is very similar to Hurker Rock (Site **14**), with its wide range of flora and fauna. The seaward or northern side of this deeply cut rock is more gradually sloping than Hurker Rock, but there are more gullies and canyons on this dive. Both rocks could be dived at the same time, but it is better to circumnavigate each rock as a separate dive.

Owing to the shape of the narrow gullies, much of the kelp forms a curtain above your head, before the rock face becomes undercut. This is the perfect place to shoot photographs up through the kelp into the sun, with perhaps a diver in the background to complete the composition. The sea bed is also made up of the shallow rocky reef, as mentioned previously, so pay particular attention to the sandy gullies between the rocky ridges, as you should be able to find razor shells and necklace shells. Sun starfish are always present, reminiscent of the crown of thorns starfish found in tropical waters.

16 Buss Craig and the Mauretana

Overall Grade – 3. *Location* – The most westerly rock of the natural breakwater protecting Eyemouth Bay, uncovered only at low tide, at 55 52 45N; 02 05 06W. *OS Grid Reference* – NT 947 651. *Average Depth* – 12m. *Typical Current Conditions* – Variable to strong. *Expertise Required* – Intermediate. *Access* – By boat only (safe anchorage from the current is provided close into the lee of the rock).

The *Mauretana*, a wood and steel steam-driven fishing vessel built in the 1930s, ran aground in thick fog on the outer edge of Hurker Rock. Before the ship could be salvaged a storm suddenly arose and wrecked her. All that remains are the huge boiler, lying at right angles to the rock, and various rusting plates, cogs and wheels that have all "welded" together with the rocky substrate. A large conger eel and an even larger lobster have been seen in the boiler – the lobster has now grown too large to be able to escape. The rocks and gullies in this area are blanketed in soft corals, sponges and anemones and are superb for photography.

Further out from Buss Craig is the start of the subterranean reef that runs all the way to the Ebb Carrs and St Abbs. The first of the submarine pinnacles is called Swearing Kate's Buss as the marks for the rock were taken from the house of Kate Swanston, well known for her foul language! This whole area is swept by a strong tidal stream, resulting in a higher than average number of marine species and making it extremely popular with divers and photographers.

Previous page: Eyemouth Bay and Killiedraughts Bay.

The *Mauretana* dramatically aground on the outer edge of Hurker Rock.

17 Luff Hard Reef

Overall Grade – 3. *Location* – Underneath Eyemouth Old Fort Point, at 55 52 42N; 02 05 18W. *OS Grid Reference* – NT 945 650. *Average Depth* – 15m. *Typical Current Conditions* – Variable to strong on the outside edge during spring tides. *Expertise Required* – Intermediate. *Access* – By boat, as the swim is too far from Eyemouth Bay.

This reef, an excellent dive site, is under the watchful eye of the Fort Point and mostly covered at high tide, but can be sized up by walking around the point at low tide. It is covered by the common mussel (*Mytilus edulis*) and the common dog whelk (*Nucella lapillus*). The far side of the reef is vertical and splits into three distinct rock groups divided by narrow canyons. These walls are covered in soft corals, anemones, starfish and nudibranchs. As you approach the reef from the sheltered, landward side, the rocks form a small canyon, the start of which is marked by an old iron anchor 3m long, the "V" of which points down into the cleft.

Debris of the wrecked steam fishing vessel *Spes-Bona* can be found here. The vessel was wrecked with all hands in October 1944, and the engine was salvaged by members of Eyemouth and District SAC in the 1960s. Continuing around to the left there are areas of large boulders strewn across the gravel sea bed, and you will eventually come to the next canyon through the reef that comes up quite shallow. Large cod and pollack will show you the way through the kelp-lined passageway.

Between this site and Little Leeds Bay (Site **18**) divers have reported finding an iron cannon in the sand. Sadly, this is not from some ancient treasure galleon but was part of the armaments from the fort on top of the headland. It was pushed over into the sea on its gun carriage in an act of vandalism many years ago.

18 Little Leeds Bay

Overall Grade – 1. *Location* – Off Northburn holiday caravan park, Eyemouth, at 55 52 45N; 02 05 36W. *OS Grid Reference* – NT 941 650. *Average Depth* – 6m. *Typical Current Conditions* – Nil. *Expertise Required* – Beginner. *Access* – By the rocky path and steps from the top of the cliff car park.

Little Leeds Bay is reached by following the footpath from the caravan park and keeping to the right along the edge of the cliff. There is a rough but usable track, with stone steps, down to the shore where entry is relatively easy, depending on the state of the tide. This is an ideal sheltered bay for trainees and the snorkelling is excellent with a profusion of life among the kelp-covered boulders.

The group of rocks that roughly cut the bay in two and face Diver's Hole (Site **20**) can easily be seen at low tide. Between the last two rocks there has formed an almost smooth-sided natural tunnel about 6m long. There are usually starfish, sea urchins and dahlia and sagartia anemones inside, and the top is fringed in a curtain of kelp. The hole is difficult to find because the entrances are shielded by kelp, but you will find it if you persevere.

By snorkelling over the end of the kelp line you will reach a sand and gravel bottom at 9m, which is usually swarming with the common hermit crab. Swimming crabs (*Liocarcinus depurator*), flounders and fifteen-spined sticklebacks (*Spinachia spinachia*) are also found here. Each side of the bay has interesting gullies and small canyons, which are home to squat lobsters and numerous species of fish. This is a great start to the diving on the north side of Eyemouth.

Above: Little Leeds Bay from the surface, and *below:* a diver exploring under the surface.

19 Hairy Ness

Overall Grade – 2. *Location* – The tip of the last headland north from Eyemouth before Coldingham Bay and St Abbs, at 55 52 46N; 02 05 37W. *OS Grid Reference* – NT 942 651. *Average Depth* – 9m. *Typical Current Conditions* – Variable, can be surge. *Expertise Required* – Beginner. *Access* – By shore from Little Leeds Bay.

This site is designated as the area from Hairy Ness Point around to Diver's Hole (Site **20**) and can be reached from Little Leeds Bay (Site **18**) or by snorkelling over Diver's Hole. Alternatively, at high tide there is a very narrow crack almost at the tip of the headland, which is best approached from the surface. Here you drop down into a circular bowl and the very narrow canyon can be traversed to the seaward edge. The wall is covered in mussels and starfish.

Just around the point at Hairy Ness there is a sand slope down to 12m and many loose boulders under which lobsters and crabs lurk. Continuing around there are several plumose anemones on a horizontal ledge. One of the most striking features about the dive is the number of dahlia anemones to be found. These occur in large aggregations and are a well-photographed feature of the dive. Swimming crabs, dragonets and the lesser octopus are commonly found here, as well as numerous species of nudibranchs, dogfish and angler fish. The dive can be terminated by returning through the crack at the point (negotiable only at high tide), swimming around to Little Leeds Bay or by continuing into Diver's Hole.

20 Diver's Hole

Overall Grade – 2. *Location* – Large cleft towards the end of Hairy Ness Point, at 55 52 46N; 02 05 37W. *OS Grid Reference* – NT 942 652. *Average Depth* – 17m. *Typical Current Conditions* – Nil in canyon, but surge to be expected. *Expertise Required* – Intermediate. *Access* – Either from Little Leeds Bay, Weasel Loch or boat.

Diver's Hole is one of the better dives at Eyemouth and can be reached by swimming all the way around from Little Leeds Bay (Site **18**) or Weasel Loch (Site **22**). The most dramatic way, however, is through the break in the headland – though this is possible only at high tide. The Little Leeds end bottoms out at 9m and by crossing through the gap in the rocks you drop down through a wave-scoured semicircular canyon to 15 to 20m, depending on the state of tide. The

The waters on the east coast, such as here at Divers Hole in Eyemouth, have a spectacular green quality.

bottom here is gravel and sand and the inner area often has an accumulation of rotting seaweed and other debris.

Here the cliff wall rises vertically on both sides and the amount of marine life to be found is astonishing. It is possible to spend an entire dive moving only a couple of metres. The 15 by 30m rock face is entirely covered with three colour variations of dead men's fingers, three variants of the elegant anemone (*Sagartia elegans nivea, miniata* and *venusta*), dahlia and plumose anemones, scorpion fish, butterfish, and twenty species of nudibranch. If you have never experienced such a wealth of life in good visibility in British waters, try diving here!

At the end of the cliff on the right-hand side the wall curves around and you travel up a steeply inclined sand slope into a shallow cave. Squat lobsters and leopard-spotted gobies dot the entire area and make superb photographic subjects. Exit by retracing your steps back through the cut or by swimming around Hairy Ness Point to Little Leeds Bay.

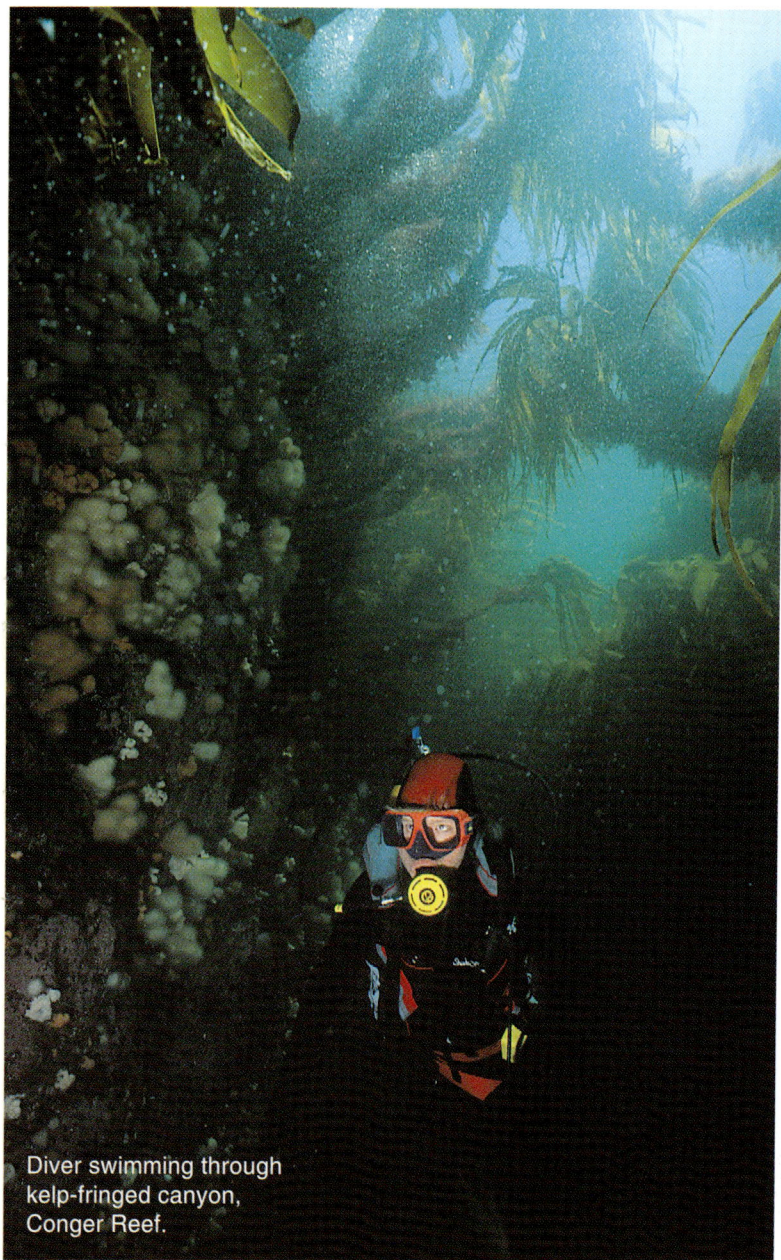

Diver swimming through
kelp-fringed canyon,
Conger Reef.

21 Conger Reef

Overall Grade – 2. *Location* – To the right from the entrance to Weasel Loch and then due north from the next headland to a raised offshore reef parallel to the shore. *OS Grid Reference* – NT 940 651. *Average Depth* – 13m. *Typical Current Conditions* – Variable, can be surge. *Expertise Required* – Beginner. *Access* – Via Weasel Loch, but can be reached by boat.

Further round to the north of Diver's Hole, the mini-wall is covered in soft corals and numerous species of anemone. The kelp forest reaches to only 8m in this area and the far wall is deeply undercut with some very large holes where conger eels and wolf fish can be found. The wolf fish, with its large interlocking front teeth, has quite a reputation for eating crabs, sea urchins and lobsters. A relative of the more common blenny, it can grow to over 1.5m in length.

When facing the cliff wall you will see a gradual slope leading up to the left; follow this up until you reach a fissure in the rock. This is the start of a narrow, winding crevice that will eventually bring you to three house-sized boulders. By working your way around them you will come back to your entry point or end up at the start of Diver's Hole (Site **20**). The boulders are covered in soft corals, anemones, hydroids and nudibranchs. At the end of this "Cresta Run", instead of turning right and swimming back to Weasel Loch (Site **22**), if you turn left at the largest of the offshore boulders (called Blind Buss) you will come onto a wide sand patch. Turn right after the sand patch and this should lead you directly into Diver's Hole (Site **20**). This dive should not be missed as there is so much marine life to see. Most divers never find the Cresta Run, though, because of the curtain of kelp that often obscures the entrance.

22 Weasel Loch

Overall Grade – 1 to 2. *Location* – Shore dive off the holiday caravan park in Eyemouth. *OS Grid Reference* – NT 939 650. *Average Depth* – 3 to 12m. *Typical Current Conditions* – Nil to slight, can be surge. *Expertise Required* – Beginner. *Access* – Directly from the shore.

Several routes can be taken to the loch other than using a boat from Eyemouth harbour. The most popular is to park on the grassy field off the caravan park and walk to the west. The cliff is about 20m high and there are sturdy wooden steps leading down to the water's edge. Weasel

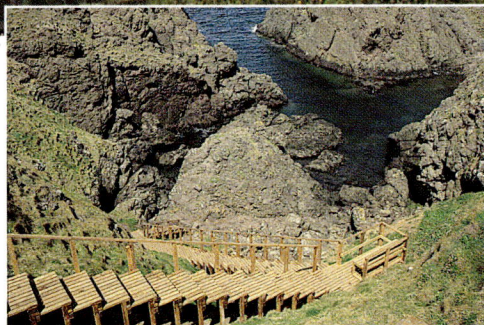

Weasel Loch (*above*) can be reached by a set of sturdy wooden steps from the caravan park at Eyemouth.

Loch, a vertical cleft cut into the rugged Berwickshire coastline, has walls lined with kelp and a sandy floor that is home to all manner of molluscs and crustaceans. Depending on the state of the tide, a brief scramble over the rocks ensures that you are suitably heated up before taking the plunge.

Large boulders are all around at first and two deep cuts at either side take you down to 6m. Here the bottom is sand-covered and the sides of the gorge are rubbed smooth by the relentless action of the sea. There are two outcrops with kelp on top and, beyond these, the wide flat sand bed has flounders, swimming crabs, dragonets and pogge. In the spring, lumpsuckers are quite common and during the full moon squid come close to shore to lay their large gelatinous eggs among the kelp fronds. This location is also excellent for snorkelling and for introducing you to the pleasures of night diving.

23 Killiedraughts

Overall Grade – 3. *Location* – Directly north, out from Weasel Loch, at 55 52 45N; 02 05 50W. *OS Grid Reference* – NT 938 650. *Average Depth* – 9 to 18m. *Typical Current Conditions* – Variable, can be surge. *Expertise Required* – Intermediate. *Access* – By shore or boat.

Although the dive is classed as being directly out from Weasel Loch (Site **22**), one of the best ways to enjoy it is by walking from the car parking area at the top of the loch around to the east, by the cliff foot path, until you come to an easy sloping entry over grass and then rocks to the sea. The dive is from this point all the way around to Weasel Loch. By keeping the rock wall to your right you will come to False Loch, similar in shape to Weasel Loch, but with a vertical wall dead end. Continue until you reach the next large entrance.

If you turn due north at this point you will travel over a field of kelp-covered boulders and small rocks until you come to a huge expanse of sand and gravel ridges. Here you will find burrowing starfish (*Astropecten irregularis*), sea potatoes (*Echinocardium cordatum*), razor shells and masked crabs (*Corystes cassivelaunus*). You should never ignore sand and gravel patches as they always have some incredibly interesting marine life forms, all of which make for great photographic subjects. Exit is by Weasel Loch.

Thornback rays are uncommon and generally found in deeper water – this one was photographed in Killiedraughts Bay.

24 Callercove Point

Overall Grade – 2. *Location* – Opposite the next large headland north in Coldingham Bay, at 55 53 00N; 02 07 00W. *OS Grid Reference* – NT 934 654. *Average Depth* – 15m. *Typical Current Conditions* – Slight, but can be surge. *Expertise Required* – Intermediate. *Access* – By boat only, from Eyemouth or St Abbs.

This rocky headland tumbles down into the water and extends considerably underwater into Coldingham Bay. Here you can find huge boulders 6m across, the tops of which are fringed in kelp and the undersides in a profusion of soft corals and anemones. There are always large shoals of pollack and saithe and the smaller boulders have families of ballan wrasse. Butterfish are common over all the rocky surfaces and Yarrell's blenny – considered quite rare in Britain – can be found regularly.

   This whole area is just a jumble of huge boulders with a gravelly and stony sea bed and is always under dived, as most visitors to the area tend to concentrate on the better-known sites. The whole of the interior edge of Coldingham Bay is similar in its rock formations and excellent dives can be found all the way along. There are hundreds of mini-walls, caverns, canyons and gullies, all of which are well worth exploring.

Callercove Point.

25 Fold Buss

Overall Grade – 3 to 4. *Location* – Offshore dive between Eyemouth and St Abbs along the outer edge of Coldingham Bay, at 55 53 18N; 02 05 30W. *OS Grid Reference* – NT 943 658. *Average Depth* – 6 to 30m. *Typical Current Conditions* – Moderate to strong. *Expertise Required* – Advanced. *Access* – By dive boat only.

This dive site is rarely visited, due to its proximity to the main shipping lanes – there are many sites much closer to the shore. Fold Buss is one of a large number of sea mounts that come to within 6 to 12m of the surface. They stretch out to form a continuous reef connecting Hurker Rock at Eyemouth with the Ebb Carrs at St Abbs. Current is to be expected, and dive leaders and boat handlers should be aware of the extra safety precautions required when visiting these offshore rocks. Diver recovery flags or SMBs should be used at all times.

Diving here is certainly spectacular, but care should be taken of boat traffic and the possibility of encountering stronger currents than expected, as the reef that peaks at Fold Buss tends to funnel the tide towards Hurker Rock. The reef is rather low lying and has a gently rolling, rocky surface covered in dead men's fingers and plumose anemones. Dotted all over it are huge dahlia anemones and Arctic bolocera anemones. Wolf fish are very common, as are squat lobsters, bottle brush hydroids (*Thuiaria thuja*) and painted topshells.

At the northern limits of the reef, before you branch inshore to the Ebb Carrs, are the remains of a German U-boat – possibly the *U-47*. Royal Navy frigates depth charged Coldingham Bay for three days in 1918 and the submarine was presumed lost at that time. Her approximate position is given on the Admiralty Chart but her location is difficult to pinpoint as the shifting sea bed tends to cover any wreckage with stones and gravel. The Horn (Site **27**) lies at the end of the reef.

ST ABBS VILLAGE TO SKELLY HOLE

Comprising the northerly part of the Marine Reserve, this incredibly rugged stretch of coastline includes the St Abbs Head nature reserve, several Sites of Special Scientific Interest and the largest number of sea caves (sub-tidal, inter-tidal and super-tidal) to be found along the south-east coast of Scotland. Over twenty-five of these caves are of particular interest to Scottish Natural Heritage and all are indicative of similar geological features to be discovered underwater. The most famous of the arches is Cathedral Rock (Site **28**) and the best tunnel, which cuts completely through a headland, is Tye's Tunnel (Site **37**).

The village of ST ABBS was once known as Coldingham Shore and was originally the closest port of call for Coldingham Priory. St Abbs Head, to the north, was previously known as Coldburgh Head and now takes its name from St Ebba, who had a nunnery on the headland. St Ebba is reputed to have disfigured herself and her nuns when the nunnery was overrun by marauding Vikings. Now St Abbs Head is better known for its wildlife reserve (see page 10). It hosts the largest number of breeding seabirds on mainland Britain and is well worth several visits, particularly during spring and early summer when the vertical cliffs are home to thousands of guillemots, seagulls, cormorants, fulmars and kittewakes.

During late June and July many of the juvenile seabirds form huge "rafts" when they first come off their nests on the precipitous cliffs. It is then that they can be approached cautiously from underwater – the birds are attracted by the air bubbles glinting in the sun and will dive down and swim around the divers under the water, an experience not to be missed. However, it should be stressed that you are not allowed to rev engines or take boats too close into the cliffs when the birds are nesting and feeding their young.

The slipway in the harbour is available for general use and small craft can be tied up securely within the harbour. Divers should check with the

Opposite: Diver on rocky wall with sea urchins at Big Green Carr (see Site **32**).

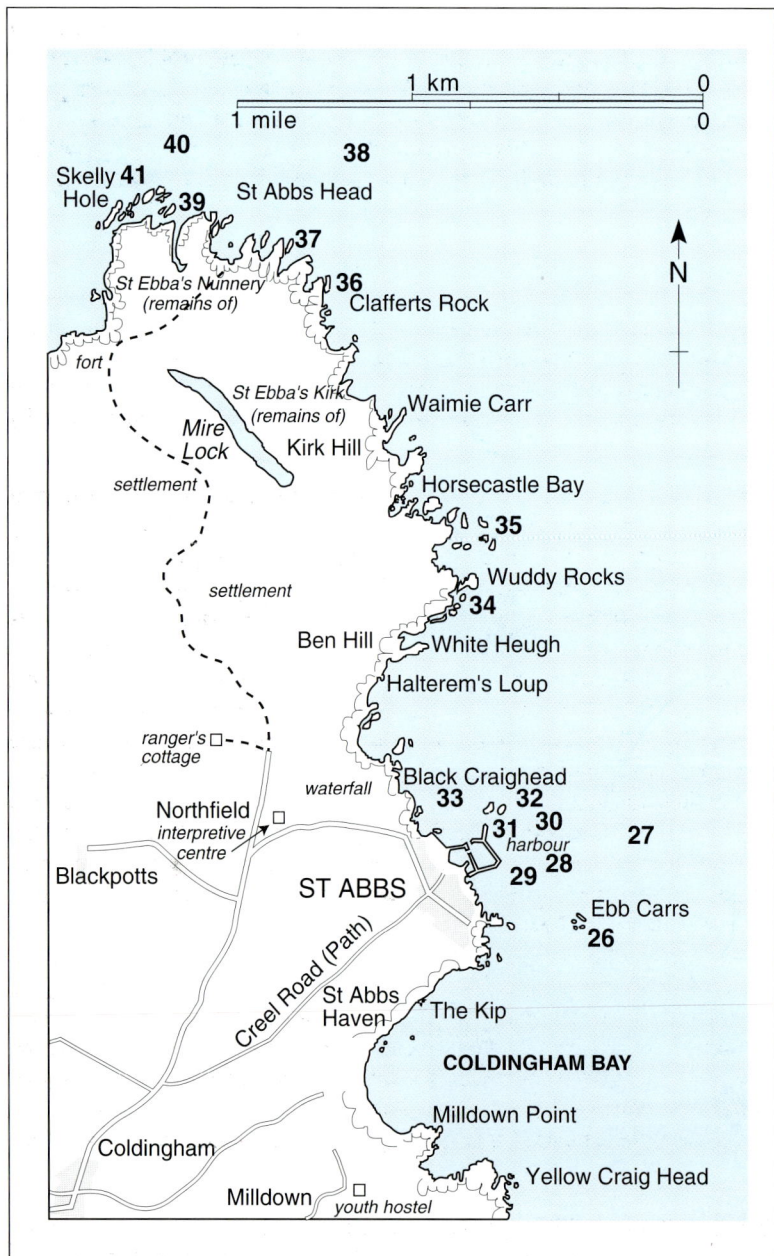

1 km 0

1 mile 0

40

38

Skelly **41**
Hole **39**

St Abbs Head

37

N

St Ebba's Nunnery
(remains of)

36

Clafferts Rock

fort

St Ebba's Kirk
(remains of)

Waimie Carr

Mire
Lock

Kirk Hill

settlement

Horsecastle Bay

35

settlement

Wuddy Rocks

34

Ben Hill

White Heugh

Halterem's Loup

ranger's
cottage

Black Craighead

waterfall

33

32

Northfield
interpretive
centre

31

30

27

harbour

Blackpotts

29 **28**

ST ABBS

Ebb Carrs

26

St Abbs
Haven

The Kip

COLDINGHAM BAY

Milldown Point

Coldingham

Yellow Craig Head

Milldown

youth hostel

72

harbourmaster (tel. 01890 771323) for costs and availability of moorings. St Abbs has been the scene of quite a few problems over the years regarding diver relations. There has often been animosity and lobster pots have been slashed or filled with rocks. In retaliation for this mindless behaviour fishermen would occupy the meagre car parking facilities with their small boats. Hopefully, much of this bad feeling has now passed.

26 The Ebb Carrs

Overall Grade – 3. *Location* – South-east of St Abbs harbour, visible from half tide, at 55 53 07N; 02 07 09W. *OS Grid Reference* – NT 924 672. *Average Depth* – 12m. *Typical Current Conditions* – Can be strong during spring tides. *Expertise Required* – Intermediate. *Access* – By boat only.

The Ebb Carrs are located at the northern end of the subterranean reef that runs all the way from Hurker Rock at Eyemouth. They are easily seen at mid tide but are completely covered at high tide. A strong current passes through the rocks and can create quite a disturbance on the surface – they should therefore only be dived during slack water (*see* the chapter on Dive Planning for information about tide times).

These rocky pinnacles rise sharply out of a gravel sea bed and form numerous interesting swimthroughs, gullies and canyons teeming with marine life. All are topped with a fringe of kelp. Dragonets are common, as are red gurnards (*Aspitrigla cuculus*). Plaice, with their pale bodies and red spots, are all over the gravel bed. Inshore from the reef, if you swim towards Thistly Briggs south of St Abbs harbour, the sea bed becomes shallower and covered in sugar kelp or dabberlocks. There is also a secondary set of small rocky pinnacles, an excellent place to find marine life.

This site contains two wrecks. The *Alfred Earlandsen* was a coastal steamer from Denmark – 207ft long, weighing 954 gross tons and carrying pit props as cargo. During a thick coastal fog, combined with rough seas, she came into Coldingham Bay to seek shelter in October 1907. Sadly, she was unaware of the Ebb Carrs being covered at high tide and was completely wrecked on 17 October, the only survivor being a dog belonging to the captain. Pit props were washed up on the shore for weeks

Opposite: St Abbs Village to Skelly Hole (Sites **26** to **41**). Wrecks in this area include the *Alfred Earlandsen* and the *Vigilant* (both at Site **26**).

Above: Peter Ray and George "Coco" Wilson, "hard-hat" divers from St Abbs, who salvaged what was left of the *Alfred Earlandsen*.

Right: The only survivor from the *Alfred Earlandsen,* the Captain's great dane.

afterwards. "Hard-hat" divers from St Abbs were able to salvage the engine from the ship, but the rest was left to the elements and is now well scattered throughout the rocky pinnacles at a depth of 12 to 15m. The first St Abbs lifeboat was the *Helen Smitten* and was launched in 1911 as a direct result of the loss of the *Alfred Earlandsen*. The lifeboat house is now home to an inshore RIB and performs a superb service along the coast.

The *Vigilant* is also testimony to the hazards of the Ebb Carrs. At just one week old, this motor fishing vessel hit the rocks during a storm, while they were submerged and blanketed in thick fog, and sank within

30 seconds in August 1977. The author was one of a team of divers who dived on her just three days after she sank. Only the steel wheelhouse remained (wrapped in ropes and netting). Finds that day included pre-packed sandwiches, aftershave lotion, bottles of aspirin, orange squash, wellington boots, oilskins, ice shovels, crushed butane gas bottles and large quantities of galvanised steel chain.

27 The Horn

Overall Grade – 2. *Location* – 220yds out from harbour wall, at 55 54 00N; 02 07 09W. *OS Grid Reference* – NT 926 711. *Average Depth* – 20m. *Typical Current Conditions* – Variable to strong, dive on a flood tide. *Expertise Required* – Intermediate. *Access* – By boat only.

The Horn is one of those excellent dives that are quite exposed when the tidal swell is running and are best dived on a flood tide during fairly calm weather. The rock walls are quite steep and cut with numerous fissures. There are dead men's fingers, plumose anemones, dahlia anemones and starfish. The sea bed is a jumble of rocks and boulders of all different sizes and gravel, creating interesting areas, almost oases, of marine life.

Thought at one time to have been the northerly end of the ridge that extends from Eyemouth, this huge boulder sits on its own and rises over 8m from the sea bed. The Horn is known for its angler fish, wolf fish, gobies, blennies, scorpion fish and many schooling species, which are attracted to this little undersea island.

28 Cathedral Rock

Overall Grade – 2. *Location* – Shore dive south of St Abbs Harbour, part of Thistly Briggs, at 55 53 55N; 02 07 29W. *OS Grid Reference* – NT 922 673. *Average Depth* – 8 to 14m. *Typical Current Conditions* – Slight to moderate. *Expertise Required* – Beginner. *Access* – Directly from the shore.

This site is famous throughout the UK; the distinctive twin arches were first dived in the early 1950s and have been on most divers' lists ever since. As well as the very large arch, there is a smaller and easily negotiable arch called the Keyhole, and the formation is reminiscent of the Twin Arches on Gozo.

The best way to find the arches is by shore dive, following the rocky reef that ends at the corner of the harbour wall. It is unnecessary – and a danger to other divers and snorkellers – to visit them by boat. The

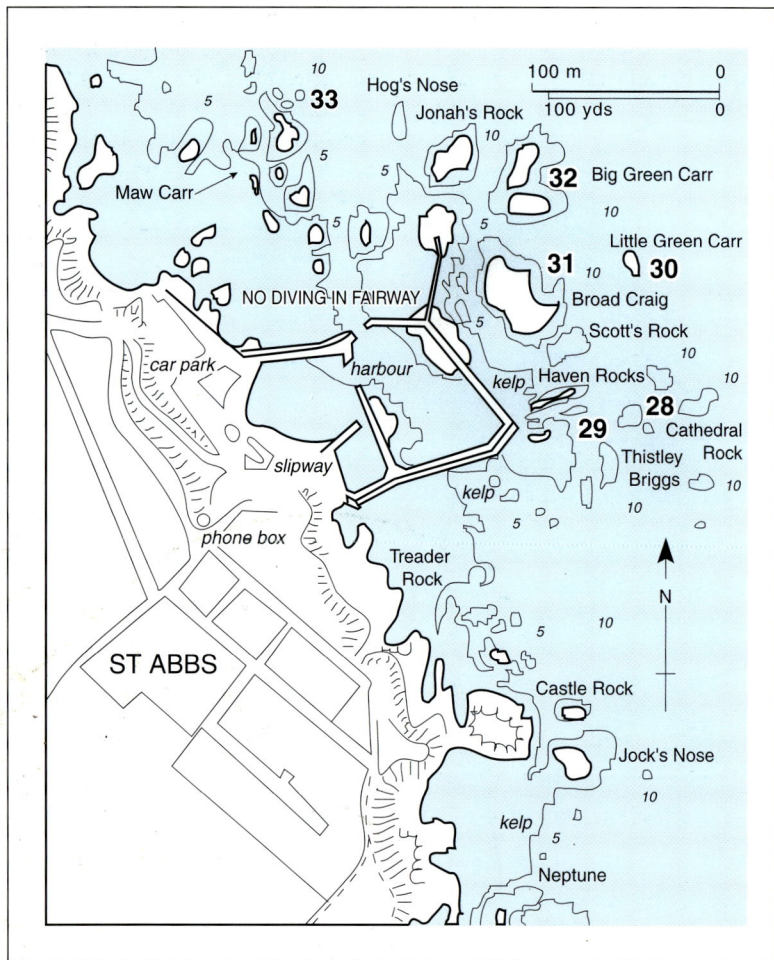

St Abbs Harbour.

easiest entry point is at the far side of the harbour wall, where it branches opposite Big Green Carr, and this is also the place to enter the water for Sites 29 to 33. Big Green Carr offers a degree of shelter from the worst waves and surge, and the sandy hole found here in 6m is often referred to as the Training Pool. Swim over to Big Green Carr; keeping it to your left swim south in the line with the reef. At the end of the reef you should see a low lying ridge extending at right angles in front of you; pass over this and you will meet a wall that curves to the left over a tumble of large boulders. With this wall to your right, you are now swimming east and you will reach Cathedral Rock in about 12 yards.

The arches have been carved out by the action of the tide and current. Because the current tends to be funnelled through them, the dive can be rather tiring during spring tides, but the compensation is the abundance of marine life and "families" of fish. There are plumose anemones, mussels, hydroids, sponges, sea cucumbers, soft corals and even cup corals. Ballan wrasse have been hand fed here over the years, making them very approachable, but please do not be tempted to chop up one of the resident sea urchins to feed to them – such behaviour is unacceptable and contravenes the conservation code for the marine reserve.

Cathedral Rock – undoubtedly one of the most famous of all British dive sites.

29 Little Amphitheatre

Overall Grade – 2. *Location* – Shore dive south of St Abbs Harbour, part of Thistly Briggs, at 55 53 54N; 02 07 30W. *OS Grid Reference* – NT 921 673. *Average Depth* – 8 to 14m. *Typical Current Conditions* – Slight to moderate. *Expertise Required* – Beginner. *Access* – Directly from the shore, but often done by boat.

Little Amphitheatre is located beyond Cathedral Rock (Site **28**) and although regarded as a shore dive, it takes a little longer to reach and is often classed as a boat dive. This is really a waste of a club's dive boat and considerably raises the risk to other divers and snorkellers in the area – use your boat sensibly for nearshore exploratory sites.

When you dive through Cathedral Rock, continue along the right-hand wall until you come to a narrow cleft in the rock that rises up into the kelp zone. Follow this cleft up and swim through the kelp for a short distance. The rock face suddenly falls away from you in a vertical drop and you should continue around to the right. You will come across a depression in the sea bed filled with rounded stones and a natural amphitheatre behind and facing you. This has been created by the pounding of the waves, which have sculpted the rock wall into numerous cracks and gullies filled with shrimps and encrusting algae,

St Abbs harbour and village.

hydroids and anemones. There are not the huge amounts of soft corals found at Cathedral Rock, but there are always large schools of pollack and saithe – they seem to be attracted into the area.

Exit is by swimming up another cleft in the rock at the right of the amphitheatre. This eventually becomes overgrown with kelp; you should continue upwards and swim over the kelp line and a very narrow ridge of rock. You will immediately be able to drop back down and return the same way back to shore as from Cathedral Rock. If you keep the wall to your left you will swim into a beautiful gully leading to the corner of the harbour wall – from here you can snorkel back to the entry point.

30 Little Green Carr

Overall Grade – 2. *Location* – Shore dive east of St Abbs Harbour, beyond Broad Craig to the outer large solitary rock, at 55 54 08N; 02 07 29W. *OS Grid Reference* – NT 923 674. *Average Depth* – 17m. *Typical Current Conditions* – Slight to moderate, can be surge. *Expertise Required* – Intermediate. *Access* – Directly from the shore.

This rock is often ignored by divers as it is considered to be too far from the shore, or just too inconvenient to reach. Entry is from the far side of the harbour, similar to the two previous sites, Cathedral Rock and Little Amphitheatre. Swim around to the left of Broad Craig (Site **31**) and continue on to Little Green Carr. This is a very large rock with steep sloping sides covered in dead men's fingers and plumose anemones.

Elegant anemones in two colour variations can be found (*Sagartia elegans nivea* and *miniata*) and many different types of sea squirts such as the light-bulb tunicate. The boulders at the bottom of the rock are also covered in soft corals and as you continue around the rock you will start to experience the flora and fauna of the offshore deeper water dive sites. There are hydroids – *Tubularia indivisa*, the sea fir *(Sertularia argentea)* and *Nemertesia antennina* – and, if you look closely, you should be able to see curious small crustaceans standing up from them. These are ghost shrimps (*Caprella linearis*) of the amphipod family; other true shrimps and prawns are also very common, such as Aesop's prawn (*Pandalus montagui*) and the common shrimp (*Crangon crangon*).

The deep-water Arctic anemone is located in the gravel patches between the rocks and, if you look closely, you will see that it has a symbiotic relationship with the common prawn, which hides under the anemone's tentacles for protection. This is an excellent dive, owing to the great diversity of species so close to the shore, and should not be missed.

31 Broad Craig

Overall Grade – 1. *Location* – First big rock facing you at the east of St Abbs harbour wall, at 55 53 56N; 02 07 32W. *OS Grid Reference* – NT 922 674. *Average Depth* – 8 to 14m. *Typical Current Conditions* – Nil to slight, mostly sheltered. *Expertise Required* – Beginner. *Access* – Directly from the shore.

Broad Craig is generally the dive site that most people first encounter when they dive at St Abbs as it is opposite the entry point for all the shore dives on the east of the harbour wall. Just to the right of the entry point is a deep pool surrounded by rocks on all sides. This is generally known as the training pool, owing to its sheltered location so close to the shore and is where most trainees get their first glimpse of North Sea marine life. The floor of the training pool is alive with hundreds of hermit crabs, continually rummaging in the kelp debris, which often collects after a storm.

Broad Craig is cut in two by a wide cleft, which allows divers to circumnavigate the rock in several directions, all of them interesting. Often it is just used as a route marker on the way to Cathedral Rock (Site **28**), or is explored on the way back from other dive sites. The seaward side of the rock is more gently sloping and covered in a forest of kelp, all of which is home to sea urchins, spider crabs and small shoals of two-spot blennies (*Gobiusculus flavescens*), which continually flit along in front of you. In the evenings these blennies will be seen resting on the kelp and are much easier to photograph.

32 Big Green Carr

Overall Grade – 2. *Location* – The largest rock to the north east of the entry point from St Abbs harbour wall, at 55 54 00N; 02 07 32W. *OS Grid Reference* – NT 922 675. *Average Depth* – 15m. *Typical Current Conditions* – Slight, but can be surge. *Expertise Required* – Beginner. *Access* – Directly from the shore.

Entry is gained from the other side of the St Abbs harbour wall. Keep to the left of the entry – Big Green Carr is the largest independent rock facing you. It is often better to snorkel the first few metres until you reach the open sand patch to the left and inshore of the rock. Keep the rock to your right and continue all the way around to bring you back to your starting point. Dive time for this full circuit is around 45 minutes.

The wall of the rock face is vertical for the most part and covered in soft corals, plumose anemones, hydroids and brittlestars. The sandy

Professor David Bellamy underwater at the Amphitheatre at
Big Green Carr (Site **32**).

surrounds always contain juvenile angler fish and there are always lots
of sea urchins and common starfish. As you approach the first turning
of the wall, swim up the shallow incline and you will discover a narrow
funnel that drops around 6m and is always fun to swim through.

Once you reach the seaward side of the rock, the first headland angles
less sharply and is covered in kelp. Keep the wall to your right and this
will bring you into the amphitheatre, with high vertical sides cut by
narrow horizontal ledges that are home to strident squat lobsters and
topknots. The rare Devonshire cup coral is found here, as is the even rarer
carpet coral (*Hoplangia durotrix*). Much of the other rock surfaces are
smothered in small tube worms (*Pomatocerous triquetor*), which will
withdraw into their tiny limescale tubes as you approach them.

Continuing around the vertical wall, there are generally lobsters to be
seen and you will soon come to a cleft in the rock that rises up and cuts
through the kelp. Swim up and through this narrow ravine and drop
back down to the sand. Again, keep the wall to your right and enjoy the
scenery as you continue back to your starting point. When you reach a
huge boulder blocking your path, turn left and surface slowly. This will
line you up with your entry at the harbour wall. This is an excellent dive
and should not be missed.

33 Maw Carr

Overall Grade – 1. *Location* – Shore dive opposite the left side of St Abbs car park, this side of harbour, at 55 54 02N; 02 07 38W. *OS Grid Reference* – NT 920 675. *Average Depth* – 8m. *Typical Current Conditions* – Nil, but can be surge. *Expertise Required* – Beginner. *Access* – Directly from the shore, an easy shore dive with some interesting and scenic views.

This is probably the easiest shore dive on the entire coast, but one dive club chose to do it as a boat dive, and anchored in the main shipping fairway! Maw Carr (also known as Seagull Rock) is two rocks with a 'split' between them. On the seaward side of the split, a cavern has been carved out by the sea and here you can find tunicates such as the sea squirt (*Ciona intestinalis*) and the light-bulb tunicate.

As this is a shallow dive the kelp plants grow all the way to the sea bed and it is only under kelp-free overhangs or in shaded areas that you can find the usual assortment of dead men's fingers and small plumose anemones. Dahlia anemones are very common on these inshore sites and come in a multitude of colours.

The Devonshire cup coral is considered quite rare along the east coast, but can be found on most dives, with careful searching.

There is a small sewage outfall close to the harbour wall. Although hardly used, it still poses a health risk, so divers should keep to the left, opposite the rock, for entry and exit.

34 Wuddy Rocks

Overall Grade – 3. *Location* – A reef that juts out from the first headland as you take a boat from St Abbs harbour to St Abbs Head, at 55 54 32N; 02 07 42W. *OS Grid Reference* – NT 921 683. *Average Depth* – 15m. *Typical Current Conditions* – Moderate, and can be surge. *Expertise Required* – Intermediate. *Access* – By boat only.

Wuddy Rocks offer a superb dive and consist of a series of huge sections of rock that jut out from the headland. Three of the largest sections are dissected by a narrow winding gully and huge archway. The best way to dive this site is by anchoring the dive boat in the sheltered bay beyond the headland known confusingly as Burnmouth Harbour. Looking towards St Abbs village, the small opening in the reef closest to shore is your starting point. Drop down to the sea bed and you will find the opening to the shaft "belled" out. Follow the smooth

Wuddy Rocks.

83

bedrock into shallower water, swim over the lip and you will find yourself descending down a very narrow shaft, the sides of which are covered in dead men's fingers. This route drops very quickly into the gloom and torches are necessary.

At the bottom there is often some kelp debris, which quickly gets stirred up. Keep the rock wall to your left and immediately turn the corner to 300°. Here you will see a huge underwater corridor in front of you. This is not strictly a tunnel because the upper rocks do not meet although they are too narrow to swim through.

This is a colossal archway that easily rivals Cathedral Rock (Site **28**) in stature, marine life and interest. If you do no other dives at St Abbs Head, do not miss this one!

35 Black Carrs

Overall Grade – 2. *Location* – Just north of Burnmouth harbour (St Abbs), the next large group of rocks beyond Wuddy Rocks, at 55 54 30N; 02 07 32W. *OS Grid Reference* – NT 922 684. *Average Depth* –

Black Carr Rocks.

Over 15m. *Typical Current Conditions* – Variable and can be surge present. *Expertise Required* – Intermediate. *Access* – By boat only.

This is essentially a tumble of huge boulders, which continue down into fairly deep water.

This is one of those disorienting dives where you and your buddy can easily get separated from the rest of your group owing to the size of the boulders and the interesting nooks and crannies to be explored. There are always wolf fish present here, as well as conger eels and the lesser octopus.

Further offshore the boulders gradually make way for a bedrock reef interspersed with sand and gravel gullies. Here the marine life differs from other inshore sites as there are more deep-water species present, particularly the Arctic anemone and the bottle-brush hydroid. It is on this distinctive hydroid that a species of isopod called *Astacilla intermedia* makes its home. This very unusual creature grows no longer than 3cm long and its young clamber up onto the parent and hang in a cluster that mimics the shape of the bottle-brush hydroid.

36 Eelcarr Rock

Overall Grade – 2. *Location* – Large rock close to the shore just south of St Abbs lighthouse, at 55 54 59N; 02 08 02W. *OS Grid Reference* – NT 915 693. *Average Depth* – 12m. *Typical Current Conditions* – Variable, but can be surge in the gully. *Expertise Required* – Beginner. *Access* – By boat only.

Eelcarr is a huge slab of rock that has become detached from the headland. It is best dived at high tide and in the morning, as are most of the St Abbs Head sites, as once the sun sinks behind the headland many of the caves and rocks can be rather gloomy and will require a torch. In the morning all the cliff faces light up and the colours displayed by the anemones and dead men's fingers are superb.

The rock is best dived from the north side where divers can approach a narrow gully that is generally a lot clearer than the open water. The base of the cleft is about 3.5m wide and the top of the sides and boulders in the shallows are covered in kelp. Continue through this channel and, by keeping the rock face to your left, you will be able to circumnavigate the rock quite easily in 30 minutes and still have plenty of air left. This is another excellent site for beginners and the photography along this stretch in the morning is superb for both close up and wide angle.

37 Tye's Tunnel

Overall Grade – 3. *Location* – Just to the north of St Abbs lighthouse, opposite Cleaver Rock at 55 55 02N; 02 08 46W. *OS Grid Reference* – NT 914 694. *Average Depth* – 6 to 20m. *Typical Current Conditions* – None in the tunnel, but can be subject to surge. Once you round the outer headland there will be moderate to strong currents depending on tidal conditions. *Expertise Required* – Intermediate. *Access* – By boat only.

The entrance to Tye's Tunnel is directly opposite a huge stack called Cleaver Rock, which is underneath the lighthouse some 30m above. Named after David Tye of Oban Divers, the narrow shaft "bells out" as you descend and the tunnel dissects the headland. The floor of the cave is filled with small smooth stones and bedrock. There being no sand nearby, the visibility is always considerably clearer than on the outside. There have been numerous landfalls during the years and one particular huge block of stone has fallen across the tunnel. This is easily negotiated and at high tide only you will be able to swim completely through to the other side into a sheltered bay. The walls of the tunnel are completely covered in small, red sea squirts, as well as the string-vest sponge (*Clathrina coriacea*), which is white. Even the scorpion fish come in shades of red and white.

Once through the cave there is a large rock facing you, which can be negotiated into quite deep water, and you will find another tunnel that cuts through this. It is best to keep the wall to your left and swim back around to the beginning of your dive, or, better still, you may retrace your route as the light is so much better for photography. This dive is not to be missed.

38 Glanmire

Overall Grade – 4. *Location* – 600yds east of St Abbs Head, at 55 55 16N; 02 08 08W. *OS Grid Reference* – NT 916 696. *Average Depth* – 30m. *Typical Current Conditions* – Variable to strong. *Expertise Required* – Advanced. *Access* – By boat only with GPS and fish finder.

The 242ft *Glanmire* struck the Black Carrs on 25 July, 1912 in thick fog. All the crew were successfully rescued but the ship came adrift and, with the aid of a strong northerly current, eventually sank just east of the St Abbs lighthouse, the bows facing the shore. Now completely

Opposite: Cleaver Rock, opposite the entrance to Tye's Tunnel.

broken up, the 1,141-ton *Glanmire* is spread over a huge area and the highest part of the flat gravel and sand sea bed is only 7m high.

This dive, first carried out on 4 September, 1965, should be undertaken only during slack water, which is around 2½ to 3hrs after high and low tide. Swept by almost continuous current, all the metal plates of the wreck are smothered in dead men's fingers and plumose

Burrowing anemones are common on deeper dive sites off St Abbs Head, including the wreck of the *Glanmire*.

anemones. Shoals of cod and the very much smaller bib or whiting (*Trisopterus luscus*) are particularly common around the wreckage. There are still bits and pieces to be found, such as the odd porthole and even the binnacle, but these should be left well alone as the wreck comes under the jurisdiction of the Marine Reserve and is protected. The sea bed surrounding the wreck is particularly interesting with burrowing anemones and the deep-water dahlia anemone.

Care must always be taken on this dive, owing to the short period of calm at slack water, and the very real danger of becoming caught in fishing line and abandoned dive boat anchor lines.

39 Headlands Cove

Overall Grade – 2. *Location* – The next very deep cut into St Abbs Head beyond Foul Carr, at 55 55 02N; 02 08 48W. *OS Grid Reference* – NT 911 695. *Average Depth* – 9m. *Typical Current Conditions* – Nil, but will have surge. *Expertise Required* – Beginner. *Access* – By boat only.

This surge gully cuts into St Abbs Head for around 55yds. It has vertical sides and a sea floor made up of smooth rounded stones on the

Razorbills dart around underwater beneath the cliffs of St Abbs Head in the constant hunt for food for the fledglings in their clifftop nests above.

inside and larger rocks and boulders covered in kelp on the outside. As it is a surge gully, the marine life on the walls is low and consists of those typical species that like turbulent water and low light. The gully is virtually always in shade as the cliff rises 60m above you. There are organ-pipe hydroids, gooseberry sea squirts and the white string-vest sponge, which is always found in association with the sea squirt.

Nudibranchs on the walls include *Limacea clavigera, Coryphella pedata, Coryphella lineata* and *Acanthodoris pilosa*. Under the kelp-topped boulders you can find velvet swimming crabs and amidst the hydroids you will find the long-legged spider crab (*Macropodia rostrata*). Sun starfish are quite common, as are dahlia anemones. This is an easy dive for beginners and photographers, away from the strong current that can sweep past the headland. On the dive you will come across seabird eggs and drowned chicks, some even being eaten by those scavengers of the shallow seas, the common starfish and the edible crab.

40 The Skells

Overall Grade – 3. *Location* – Directly out from Skelly Hole, at 55 55 03N; 02 08 47W. *OS Grid Reference* – NT 909 696. *Average Depth* – 20m. *Typical Current Conditions* – Moderate to strong. *Expertise Required* – Advanced. *Access* – By boat only.

The best entry is by anchoring the boat inside Skelly Hole (Site **41**) and swimming out through the channel and straight out to sea. As you venture out to the headland, past some huge boulders covered in soft corals, there is a small area of flat gravel sea bed swept by current, then the shelf drops away in "fingers" similar to a spur and groove reef. On the tops and sides of the ridges huge plumose anemones can be found in three colour variations, as well as thousands of brittlestars. In the valleys between can be found some of the largest dahlia anemones you will ever see, as well as angler fish and the angel shark (*Squatina squatina*).

   The sea bed at the bottom of the "finger" ridges of bedrock starts at around 20m and you would expect to use up your bottom time in this area as it is incredibly photogenic, with lots of different types of marine life to catch your interest. There is more current in this area, with a very real chance of being swept off during spring tides, and you should return the same way as you entered, seeking shelter from the current in the narrow grooves between the ridges.

41 Skelly Hole

Overall Grade – 2. *Location* – The last sheltered bay surrounded by huge rocky stacks before turning the corner to Pettico Wick Bay, at 55 54 50N; 02 08 45W. *OS Grid Reference* – NT 908 695. *Average Depth* – 12m. *Typical Current Conditions* – Slight. *Expertise Required* – Beginner. *Access* – By boat only.

Skelly Hole (sometimes referred to as Floatcarr Reef) is another superb dive site, as it has a high diversity of marine habitats and different locations where you can spend the whole day working from an anchored RIB. The main channel into the sheltered inner bay is similar to Weasel Loch at Eyemouth (Site **22**) with a wide sandy base where flounders and swimming crabs are common. The sides of the walls are mostly covered in kelp and a few soft corals, sponges and anemones, while the bottom metre is scoured clean by the constant moving of the sand in the channel during prevailing storms.

From your anchored position, following the route to the right takes you through and under two huge rock stacks. The largest, known as Floatcarr Rock, on the surface is too close to the next rock for a boat to pass through, but the underwater aspects are completely different as it "bells out". The left-hand wall is deeply sculpted and undercut with a profusion of marine life subjects to photograph and the right-hand wall, although very steep, has more dead men's fingers and anemones. The sea bed is made up of stones, which means that the water is much clearer on this side as there is less turbidity. There is also an excellent chance to swim with seabirds underneath the nesting areas.

Opposite: Diver and angler fish, Skelly Reef. Some of the angler fish here grow to a huge size.

Swimming through a
kelp-filled gully at
Skelly Hole.

PETTICO WICK TO FAST CASTLE

North of Pettico Wick much of the coastline is unexplored as most divers consider it too far to take their boats when there are so many superb dives close to St Abbs harbour. However, this under-dived and under-appreciated area is excellent and quite often contains much clearer water than that found off St Abbs, as much of the shallower sea bed is made up of bedrock in overlapping plates with gravel in between. Seals are common (because humans are not!) and the whole of the coastline appears mysterious as you sail past the rocky headlands with their dramatic vertical rock stacks, waterfalls and over twenty-five sea caves.

The whole of this stretch of coastline from Fast Castle to St Abbs harbour is dotted with caves and jutting headlands. There are sites such as Wheat Stack, Meg Watson Craig, Ermine's Heugh, Mawcarr Skells, Heatherly Carr, the wreck of the Messerschmitt Bf 110 fighter aeroplane lost in 1945, Thrummie Carr, Ebba Strand, the wrecks of the *Faraday* (lost in 1941) and the *Bear* (lost in 1891) off St Abbs Head. These sites and a dozen other headlands all offer the exploratory diver the chance of some remarkable, seldom dived sites. The wrecks, in particular, are virtually unexplored.

A number of the GPS readings were not made accurately, owing to the nature of the surrounding cliffs, so the closest point possible was taken. The readings were ratified by the Eyemouth lifeboat crew on their laser-position GPS.

42 Pettico Wick

Overall Grade – 1 to 2. *Location* – Sheltered bay facing north-west, on the north side of St Abbs Head at 55 54 49N; 02 08 45W. *OS Grid Reference* – NT 907 692. *Average Depth* – 12m. *Typical Current Conditions* – Nil to slight, depending on how far out you swim. *Expertise Required* – Beginner. *Access* – By boat or from the shore.

Overleaf: Pettico Wick to Fast Castle (Sites **42** to **50**). Wrecks in this area include the *Ringholm* (Site **43**) and the *Nyon* (Site **48**).

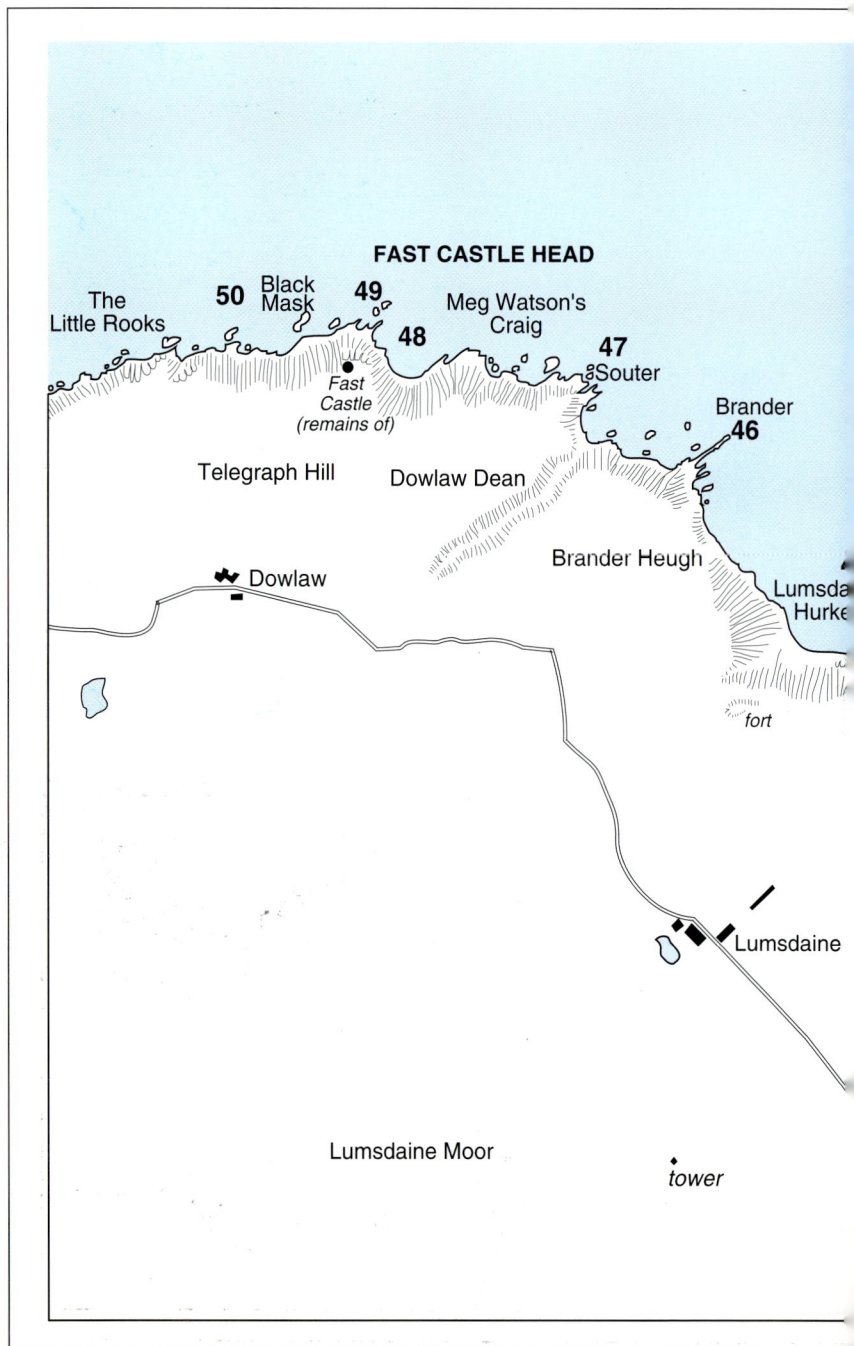

FAST CASTLE HEAD

The
Little Rooks

50 Black
Mask

49

Meg Watson's
Craig

48

47

Souter

Brander

46

Fast
Castle
(remains of)

Telegraph Hill

Dowlaw Dean

Brander Heugh

Dowlaw

Lumsda
Hurke

fort

Lumsdaine

Lumsdaine Moor

tower

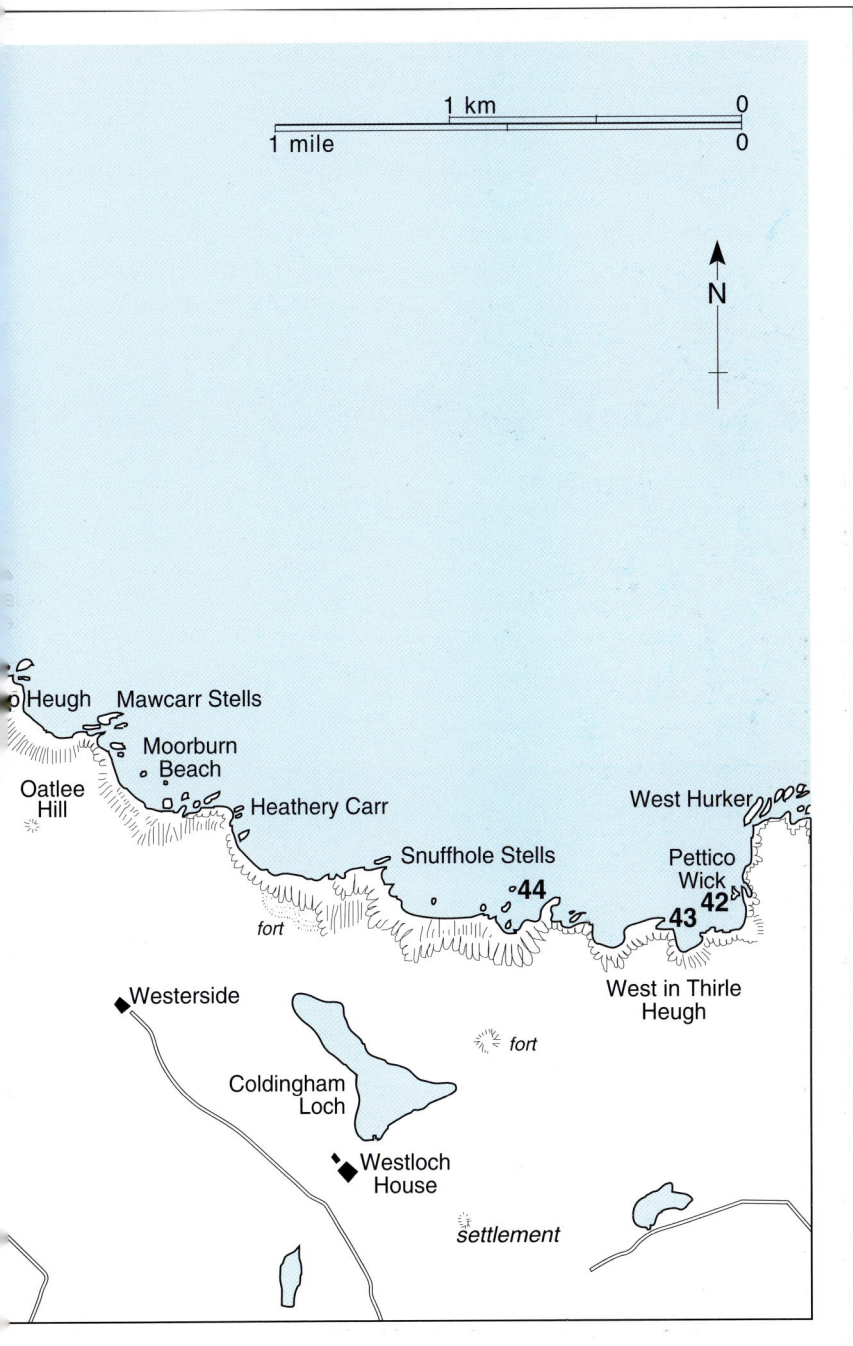

1 km   0

1 mile   0

N

Heugh   Mawcarr Stells

Moorburn
Beach

Oatlee
Hill   Heathery Carr   West Hurker

Snuffhole Stells   Pettico
44   Wick
43 **42**

fort   West in Thirle
Westerside   Heugh

fort

Coldingham
Loch

Westloch
House

settlement

Pettico Wick, to the north-west of St Abbs, has been a favourite dive site for many years as it generally offers protection from easterly winds, which can "blow out" much of the shore diving along the rest of the coast. The name is derived from a mixture of old Scots and the French influence much of the east coast of Scotland has. For many years it was called "Petty Carr Wick" or "Petite Carr Wick" – Petty meaning small, Carr meaning a rocky crag or rock and Wick meaning inlet. So the name meant "the inlet of the small rock".

The "Wick", as it is affectionately known, still has an old slipway once used by the Northern Lighthouse Board to land provisions for the St Abbs lighthouse before the road was built linking it to the village. Buildings of a former salmon fishery also stood on the sloping hillside. Sadly, over the years the bottom end of the path leading to the slipway has collapsed, making it rather difficult for divers, with all their gear, to negotiate. However, once you have achieved this, the ramp of the boat slip is robust and makes an ideal stage before you set off. Looking north-west you will see the projection of a low rock called Wick Gaut. This should be your aim for the dive and can be reached by either snorkelling or by taking a bearing of 282° magnetic and staying underwater.

On the way to Wick Gaut you will pass over an area with large stones all topped with kelp. Below 12m you will find large clumps of sea oak,

Red gurnard are a common sight around Pettico Wick.

which is home to butterfish, chameleon shrimps, mussels and several species of squat lobster and nudibranchs. The walls of Wick Gaut have strata that rise at 45° and form narrow ledges. These are home to squat lobsters, sea urchins and gobies, while the vertical parts of the wall are covered in dead men's fingers.

Keep the rock wall to your left and follow it around into shallower water. Here you will come across a small chute that cuts Wick Gaut. Further out to sea in the middle of Pettico Wick Bay the stone and gravel sea bed becomes sand and there are large numbers of hermit crabs (*Pagarus prideauxi*). This species has an association with the cloak anemone (*Adamsia maculata*), which grows completely around its shell. Red gurnards are also common in this area, as are many other sand-dwelling creatures such as burrowing starfish and large whelks (*Buccinum undatum*). The whole of Pettico Wick will suit all types of diver, and is an excellent location for snorkelling and training.

43 Ringholm

Overall Grade – 1. *Location* – Under cliff in adjoining Broadhaven Bay, west of Pettico Wick slipway, at 55 54 09N; 02 09 30W. *OS Grid Reference* – NT 906 691. *Average Depth* – 9m. *Typical Current Conditions* – Nil. *Expertise Required* – Beginner. *Access* – From the shore slipway at Pettico Wick.

The *Ringholm* was attacked by a German submarine that surfaced alongside her and ordered the crew to abandon ship. She drifted into Wester Thirle Beach at Broadhaven Bay, just west of Pettico Wick slipway. The same U-boat was responsible for sinking the trawler minesweeper *Strathrannoch* off St. Abbs Head, and was eventually sunk somewhere outside Coldingham Bay.

The *Ringholm* – sometimes referred to as the *Odense,* from her native port – was known locally for many years as the "Monkey Nut Boat" or the "Peanut Boat", owing to the loss of her cargo of peanuts when she hit the reef and sank on 15 May, 1917. Her cargo of nuts was washed up all along the Berwickshire coast for weeks after the event, and much of it was salvaged and sold at Berwick market. This coastal steamer weighed 1,756 gross tons and was over 200ft long. Now completely broken up, mostly in shallow water, her ribs and plates are covered in a lush growth of dabberlocks and oarweed.

The boilers stand upright well away from the main part of the wreckage and are surrounded by a sandy sea bed, the tops are covered in kelp. The wreckage continues out into 20m depth, where much of it is piled against a rocky ridge. The shallower parts of the wreck contain numerous wrasse, which play hide-and-seek with the divers. This dive is quite a long swim from the slipway but is excellent for snorkelling or an easy rummage dive.

44 Illustrine Gaut

Overall Grade – 3. *Location* – Second large headland past Pettico Wick Bay, at 55 55 21N; 02 11 05W. *OS Grid Reference* – NT 895 694. *Average Depth* – 12m. *Typical Current Conditions* – Variable, can be surge. *Expertise Required* – Intermediate. *Access* – By boat only.

The shore side of this rock is very dramatic with vertically rising cliffs and a tumble of boulders at the bottom. The sea bed slopes away under these boulders, which are covered in kelp and sea urchins, and gradually the bedrock slopes off in great sheets of stone with narrow ridges and cracks in between. The flat sheets of rock are quite featureless but where a crack has formed there is an oasis of life with hydroids, sea squirts, dead men's fingers and nudibranchs.

The rocks are grazed heavily by sea urchins so there is little algal growth. Once you reach around 18m the bedrock gradually gives way to rocky ridges interspersed with gravel. This now takes on much the same type of features as The Skells (Site **43**) with the rocky ridges topped with dead men's fingers, plumose anemones and dahlia anemones, and the gravel patches absolutely alive with brittlestars of at least three different varieties. These are *Ophiocomina niger, Ophiothrix fragilis* and the very much smaller *Ophiura ophiura*, all of which are preyed upon by the sun starfish. The gravel beds also have some particularly interesting crustaceans, such as several species of shrimp and prawn and the circular crab (*Atelecyclus rotundatus*). This is an excellent site for trainees, as the location is also close to quite deep water.

45 Lumsdaine Hurker

Overall Grade – 2. *Location* – 4 miles north of St Abbs Head, at 55 55 42N; 02 12 04W. *OS Grid Reference* – NT 878 704. *Average Depth* – 12m. *Typical Current Conditions* – Slight, but can be surge close into the rocks. *Expertise Required* – Intermediate. *Access* – By boat only.

Lumsdaine Hurker is a large, solitary boulder set back approximately 110yds from Lumsdaine Beach. The cliff headland that juts out also has a small tumble of boulders and a rocky reef at its base, and deep water

Left: Northern prawns are common on all deeper dives. *Below:* Scampi prawns (*Nephrops norvegicus*).

Left: The common prawn is often difficult to spot as it hides on or under the fine gravel or sand sea bed.

can be found all the way into the gravel shore, making it ideal for securing the boat onto the reef and enjoying a mid-dive break. The undersea strata has also formed a dyke, which juts out from the headland and forms the north side of a ridge running parallel with the strata on the shore. The walls of Lumsdaine Hurker at first sight are quite sparse, apart from the top fringe of kelp, mussels and barnacles, but below this can be found dead men's fingers, dahlia anemones, various sponges and tiny gooseberry sea squirts. The sea bed, made up of sand, gravel and well-worn rounded stones, gradually makes way for a boulder bed, which coincides with the bedrock extending onto the beach.

The boulders are all topped with kelp and the sides covered in soft corals and anemones. Ballan wrasse are common, as are flounders, saithe, pollack and cod. Continuing seaward, the boulders gradually give way to a wide-ridged sand and gravel sea bed where angler fish can be found. The egg cases of the lesser-spotted dogfish (*Scyliorhinus canicula*) have also been found at this site.

Lumsdaine Hurker is best dived on a flood tide, to allow a degree of safety if you are swept into the next bay.

46 Brander

Overall Grade – 2. *Location* – North of St Abbs Head to huge outcrop of vertical rock strata before Fast Castle Head, at 55 54 49N; 02 11 33W. *OS Grid Reference* – NT 874 707. *Average Depth* – 12m. *Typical Current Conditions* – Slight, but can be surge close into the rocks. *Expertise Required* – Intermediate. *Access* – By boat only.

You cannot miss Brander as you motor north to Fast Castle Head. It is a huge rocky dyke that juts out from the shore, and its strata have all been turned to 75° (or are nearly vertical in some places). The dyke extends out underwater to 27m, where it disappears into a gravel sea bed, featureless except for millions of brittlestars. Most divers ignore these gravel beds although along this under-dived stretch of coast you will find sea cucumbers, feather starfish, sand mason worms, gobies, blennies and interesting hydroids, fish and sponges.

By keeping the rocky face to your left you can swim out along the undercut headland, which extends underwater, and follow it around into the next bay. This north-west side of the headland is more sheer, and although it gets less light than the other side it is still covered in soft corals, anemones and starfish. There are ballan wrasse everywhere but they are mostly shy of divers. During the spring you often see lumpsuckers, which are preyed upon by seals, in among the shallow boulders. Although seals are quite rare along the coast, they are noted around a few of the shallower inlets off St Abbs Head and are always a delight to find. However, divers rarely catch sight of them underwater here – an experience enjoyed further north at Bass Rock, or to the south off the Farne Islands.

47 Souter

Overall Grade – 2. *Location* – Large prominent rock stack set back from the cliffs, towards Fast Castle Point, amidst lots of vertical rock strata and dotted with sea caves, at 55 55 55N; 02 12 29W. *OS Grid Reference* – NT 869 709. *Average Depth* – Over 15m. *Typical Current Conditions* – Variable and can be surge. *Expertise Required* – Intermediate. *Access* – By boat only.

This huge rock stack is 3 miles north along the coast from Pettico Wick. Although it is a very obvious landmark, all of this stretch of coast is little dived as most people consider it too far to take their dive boats, with so many excellent sites closer to St Abbs. The scenery of Souter is just as dramatic underwater as it is above the surface, with huge boulders and sandy canyons. The shallower boulders are covered in a lush growth of kelp and there appear to be more spider crabs clinging onto the undersides of the kelp in this area, as well as more edible crabs.

There are numerous nudibranchs, as well as shrimps, mussels, scorpion fish, butterfish, soft corals and huge dahlia anemones. Below the 15m mark you come into huge carpets of brittlestars, sun starfish and deep-water hydroids. Although the terrain and marine life are similar to those of the rest of this under-dived stretch, they appear different because of the different shapes and structure of the bedrock and the larger numbers of fish found. Approximately 110yds south of Souter Point are the remains of an ancient sailing ship, including an anchor with its chain, a rudder and a brass compass embedded in the rocks. Again, this dive is best done on a flood tide.

48 Nyon

Overall Grade – 2. *Location* – 4 miles north of St Abbs Head, at 55 55 56N; 02 12 52W. *OS Grid Reference* – NT 866 710. *Average Depth* – 9m. *Typical Current Conditions* – Slight, but can be surge. *Expertise Required* – Beginner. *Access* – By boat only.

The 4,950-ton Swiss motor vessel *Nyon*, on its way from Leith to Dakar, struck Meg Watson's Rock near Fast Castle, 4 miles north of St Abbs Head on 17 November, 1958. The following day the St Abbs branch of the Board of Trade Life Saving Association made a daring rescue by firing a line by rocket from the cliff tops over to the *Nyon*. The crew were able to attach a steel hawser, which was then pulled back up the cliffs and attached to a tripod (no longer there). A breeches buoy was then lowered to the ship and eventually all the crew were rescued. Meanwhile, the St Abbs lifeboat, manned by Coxswain James Wilson, established an RNLI record by standing by at the scene of the wreck from 18 to 27 November and, after picking them up from the shore, finally landed the crew and all their belongings at St Abbs harbour.

Three tugboats from North Shields were unsuccessful in pulling the *Nyon* off the rocks and the ship had to be abandoned. Some time later a salvage operation was mounted and the stern section of the ill-fated ship was cut off and towed to Rotterdam, where she was fitted with a new front part and bow. Sadly, this section of the ship also came to grief when she was sunk after a collision near Beachy Head.

The now abandoned forepart of the ship was left to the elements and was soon broken up by the inevitable winter storms that frequent the

The SS *Nyon* aground on Meg Watson's Rock, with the St Abbs Board of Trade Life Saving Association in attendance.

coast. Parts of the wreckage can be seen at low tide jutting up among the tangle of boulders on the shore. Spread over a wide area this is very much a rummage dive, as the girders and plates are jumbled among kelp-covered rocks and, for the most part, are completely overgrown with kelp and other seaweeds. The best of the diving is below the kelp line at around 9m, where the boulders open out into bedrock and more of the wreckage can be seen.

49 Fast Castle

Overall Grade – 2. *Location* – 4 miles north of St Abbs Head, at 55 55 59N; 02 13 07W. *OS Grid Reference* – NT 862 711. *Average Depth* – 12m. *Typical Current Conditions* – Slight, but can be surge close into the rocks. *Expertise Required* – Intermediate. *Access* – By boat only.

Fast Castle, the setting for Sir Walter Scott's *Bride of Lammermuir*, was a castle stronghold belonging to the Home family. This isolated castle, often known as "Wolf's Crag" or "Castle Rock", has seen history being made within her ancient walls. Mary Queen of Scots was incarcerated there for a short time, and the failed assassination attempt on King James IV was hatched and carried out by its then owner, the Earl of Gowrie. Fast Castle was also reputed to have had a fortune in Spanish gold hidden in a cave beneath its cliffs! Eyemouth and District SAC were the first divers to explore the area on 24 September, 1967 – and they did so again on 27 April, 1969 accompanied by a BBC film crew.

Unfortunately, these first exploration attempts were hampered by strong surge conditions within the cave and in water of around only 1m in depth. The cave sides are worn into potholes and smoothed off by the constant pounding of the waves but the top of the cave is so high that you need strong torches to be able to explore further. At the entrance of the cave an underwater shaft was discovered 6m down, which appeared to be the source of a freshwater spring but yielded no sign of any treasure, just a fine silt and kelp debris that quickly reduced the visibility and prevented further exploration. This is still very much unexplored territory and there is much good diving to be had along these offshore reefs and headlands.

50 The Rooks

Overall Grade – 2. *Location* – 4 miles north of St Abbs Head, at 55 54 12N; 02 07 47W. *OS Grid Reference* – NT 853 710. *Average Depth* – 12m. *Typical Current Conditions* – Slight, but can be surge close into the rocks. *Expertise Required* – Intermediate. *Access* – By boat only.

The Rooks is a series of massive rocks that have become separated from the headland but are joined by bedrock underwater, interspersed with gravel beds. Completely under water, the channels around the rocks have been eroded away over the centuries to create several distinct passages into the more sheltered inner area of inter-tidal rocks and gullies. The bay itself is quite shallow, with an average depth of only 6m, and is covered in boulders all topped with kelp. There are a couple of open sandy patches, which can be seen quite clearly from the top of the cliff.

The passageways between the rocks are near vertical sided and covered in dead men's fingers, hydroids, sponges and anemones. Further south there are numerous other large solitary boulders, all of them worth exploring. This is generally as far as any of the dive boats venture from St Abbs. During January and February it is a favourite location for diving with seals, and dozens of juveniles can be seen sheltering on the rocky shoreline. There are many seals in this area, on account of there being very little human intervention.

APPENDIX 1: DIVE SERVICES

The information given here was correct and relevant (although not exhaustive) at the time of print, but the author and publishers would greatly appreciate any new information regarding services, which may be used, with acknowledgement, when this guide is updated.

Dive centres and dive schools

AquaNorth, 17A Coast Road, Newcastle upon Tyne NE7 7RN (tel./fax 0191 266 6626). PADI Instructor Development Centre; equipment sales and rental; boat hire; air.

Blue Dolphin Scuba Centre, 32 Montrose Terrace, Abbeyhill, Edinburgh EH7 5DL (tel. 0131 666 3321; fax 0131 652 2660). PADI school; equipment sales and rental; boat hire, air and enriched air.

Cromwell Marine, Old Harbour, Dunbar, East Lothian (tel. 01368 863354). Equipment sales; air.

The Diving Centre, 41 Bath Lane, Newcastle upon Tyne NE4 5SP (tel. 0191 232 7983; fax 0191 261 4948). PADI Instructor Development Centre; equipment sales and rental; boat hire; air.

Edinburgh Diving Centre, 1 Watson Crescent, Edinburgh EH11 1HD (tel. 0131 229 4838; fax 0131 622 7099). BSAC and PADI school; equipment sales and rental; boat hire; air.

Eyemouth Diving Centre, Fort Road, Eyemouth TD14 5ES (tel./fax 01890 751202 and 01289 302893; e-mail eyedivecen@aol.com). BSAC and PADI school; equipment sales and rental; boat hire; air and enriched air.

Farne Diving Services, Beadnell, Northumberland NE67 5AP (tel./fax 01665 720615). Equipment sales and rental; boat hire; air.

Lodge, 146 Main Street, Seahouses, Northumberland NE68 7UA (tel. 01665 720158). Equipment sales and rental; boat hire; air.

Opposite: St Abbs village car park with Seagull Rock behind.

Ocean Eye Films, 1 The Clouds, Duns, Berwickshire TD11 3BB (tel. 01361 882628; fax 01361 882975; e-mail lawson@oceaneye. demon.co.uk). Underwater photographic workshops and tuition.

Scoutscroft Diving Centre, Coldingham, Berwickshire TD14 5NB (tel. 01890 771338; fax 01890 771746; e-mail scoutscroft@compuserve. com). PADI school; equipment sales and rental; boat hire; air.

Splashsports Services Edinburgh, Unit 26, West Gorgie Park, Hutchison Road, Edinburgh EH14 1UT (tel. 0131 455 8788; fax 0131 455 8787). PADI school; equipment sales and rental; boat hire; air.

Dive charter boats

Charter Ribs, Tyneside (tel. 0191 297 0914). RIBs of various sizes for hire to dive clubs, fully kitted out including trailer and engine.

MV *Guiding Star*, P. Gibson, The Rest, St Abbs (tel. 01890 771681). Licensed for twelve divers.

MV *Promised Land*, Seahouses (tel. 01665 720938). Skipper Chris Hall; 10m MFV licensed for twelve divers.

MV *Restless Wave*, J. Johnston, Burnmouth (tel. 01890 781370); 10m MFV licensed for twelve divers.

MV *Sovereign II* and MV *Sovereign III*, Seahouses (tel. 01665 720059). Owner Ian Douglas; 12m Aquaster and 12m Cheverton "pilot boats" each licensed for twelve divers.

MV *Wave Dancer* and MV *Wave Dancer II*, Seahouses (tel. 01665 720892). Owner Colin Rutter; 10m MFVs each licensed for twelve divers.

MFV *Harvest Home*, Seahouses (tel. 01665 720832). Skipper Billy Lawrence; 9m Halmatic MFV licensed for twelve divers.

Many other day charter boats are available from all the harbours and are easy to organise.

Diving clubs

Berwick and District Sub-Aqua Club, c/o Michael Avril, 14 Islestone Court, Tweedmouth TD15 2DT (tel. 01289 308685). Members of the Sub-Aqua Association.

Berwickshire Sub-Aqua Club, c/o John Goldie, The Bield, St Abbs Road, Coldingham TD14 5NR (tel. 01890 771515). Members of the Scottish Sub-Aqua Club.

British Sub-Aqua Club, Telford's Quay, Ellesmere Port, South Wirral L65 4FY (tel. 0151 357 1951; fax 0151 357 1250).

East Lothian Sub-Aqua Club, c/o John Cowan, Gardeners Bothy, Whittingham Estate, Haddington, East Lothian (tel. 01368 850694). Members of the Scottish Sub-Aqua Club.

Eyemouth and District Sub-Aqua Club, c/o Alec Struthers, 1 Douglas Crescent, Longniddry EH32 0LH. Independent club.

Handicap Scuba Association International, 63 Farleigh Crescent, Lawn Estate, Swindon, Wiltshire SN3 1JY (tel./fax. 01793 695479).

Kelso Sub-Aqua Club, c/o Monica Kerr, Hazelbank, 35 Wheatland Road, Hawick TW9 3NW. Members of the Scottish Sub-Aqua Club.

PADI International, Unit 6, Unicorn Park, Whitby Road, Bristol, Avon BS4 4EX (tel. 0117 971 1717; fax 0117 971 0400).

Scottish Sub-Aqua Club, 40 Bogmoor Place, Glasgow G51 1BR (tel./ fax 0141 425 1021).

Sub-Aqua Association, Northern House, 43-45 Pembroke Place, Liverpool L3 5PH (tel./fax 0151 707 0111).

APPENDIX 2:
THE DIVER'S CODE OF CONDUCT

Divers should at all times adhere to the BSAC code of conduct. It is reproduced here with the kind permission of the British Sub-Aqua Club, and has been extracted from the BSAC *Safe Diving Practices* booklet, available from BSAC Headquarters.

THE DIVER'S CODE OF CONDUCT

More and more people are taking to the water. Some for recreation; some to earn their living. This code is designed to ensure that divers do not come into conflict with other water users. It is vital that you observe it at all times.

Before leaving home

Contact the nearest British Sub-Aqua Club Branch or the dive operator local to the dive site for their advice. Seek advice from them about the local conditions and regulations.

On the beach, river bank or lakeside

1. Obtain permission, before diving in a harbour or estuary or in private water. Thank those responsible before you leave. Pay harbour dues.
2. Try to avoid overcrowding one site, consider other people on the beach.
3. Park sensibly. Avoid obstructing narrow approach roads. Keep off verges. Pay parking fees and use proper car parks.
4. Don't spread yourselves and your equipment since you may upset other people. Keep launching ramps and slipways clear.
5. Please keep the peace. Don't operate a compressor within earshot of other people – or late at night.

Opposite: Diver examining marine life in Weasel Loch.

6. Pick up litter. Close gates. Be careful about fires. Avoid any damage to land or crops.

7. Obey special instructions such as National Trust rules, local bye-laws and regulations about camping and caravanning.

8. Remember divers in wetsuits are conspicuous and bad behaviour could ban us from beaches.

In and on the water

1. Mark your dive boats so that your Club can be identified easily. Unmarked boats may become suspect.

2. Ask the harbour-master or local officials where to launch your boat – and do as they say. Tell the Coastguard, or responsible person, where you are going and tell them when you are back.

3. Stay away from buoys, pots, and pot markers. Ask local fishermen where not to dive. Offer to help them recover lost gear.

4. Remember ships have not got brakes, so avoid diving in fairways or areas of heavy surface traffic and observe the "International Regulations for the Prevention of Collisions at Sea".

5. Always fly the diving flag when diving, but not when on the way to, or from, the dive site. Never leave a boat unattended.

6. Do not come in to bathing beaches under power. Use any special approach lanes. Do not disturb any seal or bird colonies with your boats. Watch your wash in crowded anchorages.

7. Whenever possible, divers should use a surface marker buoy.

On conservation

1. Never use a speargun with an aqualung. Never use a speargun in fresh water.

2. Shellfish, such as crabs and lobsters, take several years to grow to maturity; over-collecting in an area soon depletes stocks. Only take mature fish or shellfish and then only what you need for yourself. Never sell your catch or clean it in public or on the beach. Don't display your trophies. [Author's note: This paragraph does not apply to the Berwickshire coast, the whole of which is designated as a Special Area of Conservation. The collection of shellfish by divers will not be tolerated.]

3. Be conservation conscious. Avoid damage to weeds and the sea bed. Do not bring up sea-fans, corals, starfish or sea urchins – in one moment you can destroy years of growth.

4. Take photographs and notes – not specimens. Shoot with a camera not a speargun – spearfishing makes fish shy of divers. Never spearfish wrasse or other inshore species since once an area is depleted of such fish, it may take a long time for them to re-colonise.

On wrecks

1. Do not dive on a designated wreck site. These are indicated on Admiralty Charts and marked by buoys or warning notices on the shore nearby.

2. Do not lift anything which appears to be of historical importance.

3. If you do discover a wreck, do not talk about it. Pinpoint the site, do a rough survey and report it to the BSAC Archaeology Adviser and the Council for Nautical Archaeology who will advise you.

4. If you do not lift anything from the wreck, it is not necessary to report your discovery to the Receiver of Wreck. If you do lift, you must report.

5. If your find is important, you may apply for it to be designated a protected site. Then you can build up a well qualified team with the right credentials and proceed with a systematic survey or excavation under licence without outside interference.

Don't Let Divers Down – Keep To The Diver's Code

APPENDIX 3: FURTHER READING

It is almost impossible to write an original book on marine life and scuba diving and the author is indebted to all those publications that line his shelves. Readers might find the following useful for further study:

British Sea Fishes, Dr Frances Dipper, Underwater World Publications, Teddington, 1987.

BSAC Wreck Register No 5 – Scotland, W.E. Butland, J.K. Siedlecki and C. Riley, BSAC.

Dive Scotland Volume III, Gordon Ridley, Underwater World Publications, Teddington, 1992.

The Diver's Guide to the North-East Coast, Peter Collings, Collings & Brodie, 1986.

Field Guide to Nudibranchs of the British Isles, Bernard Picton, Immel Publishing, London, 1994.

Field Guide to Shallow water Echinoderms, Bernard Picton, Immel Publishing, London, 1993.

Guide to St Abbs and Eyemouth Marine Reserve, Carol Warman, 1987.

Hamlyn Guide to Seashore and Shallow Seas of Britain and Europe, Hamlyn, 1979.

Marine Conservation Society Guide to the Sea Life of Britain and Ireland, Immel Publishing, London, 1988.

Marine Life, David and Jennifer George, Harrap, 1979.

Marine Life, De Haas and Knorr, Burke, 1966.

Undersea Britain, Rob Palmer, Immel Publishing, London, 1990.

Walks,Whelks and Wolf-fish, George Davidson & Peter Tinsley.

Opposite: A tiny hermit crab amid soft corals and sea squirts.

ACKNOWLEDGEMENTS

This book is a culmination of over thirty years of diving along the Berwickshire coastline, in particular off my home town of Eyemouth. It is impossible to list all the help I have received over the years, but I should like to make some notable exceptions.

Andy Collin, Jim Martin and Tom Bell, early pioneers of Eyemouth and District SAC, who took me on my first dive. The Berwickshire branch of the Scottish SAC – my local dive club. The Marine Conservation Society, Scottish Wildlife Trust, National Trust for Scotland, Scottish Natural Heritage, Stephen and Carol Warman, Ralph Holmes, George Davidson, John Goldie, Kevin Rideout and Fiona Crouch. My thanks to Alistair Crowe and the crew of the St Abbs inshore lifeboat. The crew of the Eyemouth lifeboat. John Parkin of the Eyemouth Diving Centre. Tim Marchant.

My mother, Barbara, who used to worry so much when I first started diving (and still does). My father, Rob, who encouraged the formation of the first ever marine reserve in Scotland – Barefoots, at Eyemouth. My daughter, Lindsay, and son, Jamie, who have grown to be fine divers. Last but by no means least my wife, Lesley, and our daughter, Emma, and grand-daughter, Rebecca, who collectively have all had to put up with my absence whilst pursuing a passion, the St Abbs and Eyemouth Voluntary Marine Nature Reserve.

All the colour photographs were taken by the author, with the exception of the portrait of the author on the outside back cover which was taken by Lesley Orson. The black-and-white photographs on page ii and 74 (top) were supplied by R. and M. Thomson; pages 48 and 59 by the Eyemouth Museum; page 74 (inset) is taken from a postcard from John Woods of Coldingham; and the photograph on page 102 by R. Nisbet.

Opposite: Vertical walls and gullies are very much a feature of diving around St Abbs and Eyemouth.

INDEX

The bold numbers in parentheses are dive site numbers.

Opposite: The feeding polyps of dead men's fingers clearly show their resemblance to the anemone and true coral family. Here, they can be seen with collected food particles.

view